Chapters
from
Ancient History

Chapters from Ancient History

compiled by
Dorothy Harrer

Waldorf
PUBLICATIONS
RESEARCH INSTITUTE FOR Waldorf EDUCATION

Printed with support from the Waldorf Curriculum Fund

Published by:

Waldorf Publications at the
Research Institute for Waldorf Education
38 Main Street
Chatham, NY 12037

Title: *Chapters from Ancient History*
Author: Dorothy Harrer
Copy editor/proofreader: Meg Gorman
Layout: Ann Erwin
Cover image: *Villa of the Mysteries*, fresco, Pompeii

Contents

Ancient India

The whole Veda is the first source
Of the sacred law. Whatever law
Has been ordained for any person
By Manu, that has been fully
Declared in the Veda.

Rich in royal worth and valor,
Rich in holy Vedic lore,
Dasaratha ruled his empire
In the happy days of yore –
Like the ancient monarch Manu,
Father of the human race,
Dasaratha ruled his people
With a father's loving grace –
Twice-born men were free from passion,
Lust of gold and impure greed,
Faithful to their rites and scriptures,
Truthful in their word and deed –
Kshatriyas bowed to holy Brahmans,
Vaisyas to the Kshatriyas bowed,
Toiling Sudras lived by labor,
Of their honest duty proud.
　　　– The Rig Veda

This is the noble truth
Concerning the way which leads
To the destruction of sorrow:
Verily! It is the noble eightfold path;
That is to say:
Right discrimination, right judgment,
Right speech, right deed,
Right relationship, right effort,
Right memory thoughts, right balance.
　　　– Gautama Buddha

In ancient India
men looked upon
this world as
unreal or *maya*.
They longed to return
to the real world
of heaven
where all was real
and everlasting,
and they considered
life on earth
to be a time
in which to prepare
for a return
to Brahma.

Song of Creation

from the *RIG VEDA*
(Sanskrit, three verses, and English)

NASAD ASIN, NA SAD ASIT TADANIM:
There was not non-existent nor existent:

NASID RAJO NO VIOMA PARO YAT.
There was no realm of air, no sky beyond it.

KIM AVARIVAH? KUHA? KASYA SARMANN?
What covered in and where? And what gave shelter?

AMBA KIM ASID, GAHANAM, GABIHIRAM?
Was water there, unfathomed depth of water?

NA MRYTUR ASID, AMRITAM MATACHI,
Death was not then, nor was there aught immortal,

NA RATRIA AHUA ASIT PRAKETRA.
No sign was there, the day's and night's divider.

ANID AVATAM SVADHAYA TAD EKAM,
That one thing, breathless, breathed by it own nature,

TASMAD DHANYAN NAPARAH KIM CANASA.
Apart from it was nothing whatsoever.

TAMA ASIT TAMASA GULHAM AGRE;
Darkness there was; at first concealed in darkness;

APRAKITAM SALIKAM SARVAM A IDAM.
This All was indiscriminate chaos.

TUCHYENABHU APIHITAM YAD ASIT,
All that existed then was void and formless,

TAPASAS TAN MAHINAJAYAT AIKAM.
By the great power of warmth was born that Sole One.

Who verily knows, and who can here declare it,
  whence it was born and whence comes this creation?
The gods are later than this world's production,
  who knows, then, whence it first came into being?

He, the first origin of this creation,
  whether he formed it all, or did not form it,
Whose eye controls this world in highest heaven,
  he verily knows it, or perhaps he knows not.

Help with the Sanskrit words and their pronunciation was received from A. Bhadkamkar of Bombay. All *A*s are pronounced "ah." The *H*s after consonants are sounded forth as in "d-ha-yan" and "tuchyena-b-hu." The *G*s are as in "good" or "grand." This English translation is taken from *Hindu Scriptures*, edited by Nicol Macnicol and published by Everyman's Library, E.P. Dutton, New York.

The Creation and the Flood

In the beginning there was no life, no lifelessness, no air, no sky, no sign dividing day from night. The universe existed in the shape of darkness, wholly immersed, as it were, in deep sleep. Then the divine Self-existent appeared with irresistible power, dispelling the darkness. He who contains all beings shone forth of his own will.

Desiring to produce beings of many kinds, He created the waters and breathed warmth into them. He placed His seed in them, and that seed became a golden egg more brilliant than the Sun. And in that egg, He, Himself, was born as Brahma, the progenitor of the whole world.

He rested in the egg for a whole year. Then, by his thought, He divided the egg into two halves. Out of these two halves, He formed the heaven and the earth, between them the middle sphere, the eternal abode of the waters.

By the breath of his mouth, He created the gods who entered the sky. And by breathing downward He created the demons, thus separating good from evil, light from darkness. For with the creation of the gods shone the day, and with the creation of the demons came darkness.

Then for the sake of the prosperity of the worlds, He caused the priests to proceed from His mouth, the warriors from His arms, the merchants from His thighs, and from His feet, those men who were to labor as servants of others.

He then divided His own body into two parts, male and female, and brought forth a son, Virag, who became the father of Manu who was called The Child of the Sun, the First King of Men, for to him Brahma revealed the Sacred Laws as to how human beings were to live on earth.

Four great ages, or epochs of time, followed the creation of the world and of mankind. In the Krita Yuga, or the Perfect Age, all men were saintly and without fear, without pride or hatred. Their minds were constantly full of delight, for they could see heaven and the spiritual beings who guided the world. And they felt themselves to be brothers, the children of Brahma, their Creator. They said, "We live in and are a part of Brahma." The weather was neither too warm nor too cold. There were no houses of any kind. Nor were there plants.

All mankind's needs were supplied without his having to make any effort. Men never grew old although they lived for four thousand years. They were never sick, nor did they suffer harmful accidents. Once in a lifetime, children were born to them in pairs, out of their thought. When at last they died, other men descended from heaven to take their places.

Then began a new age, the Treta Yuga, which was less perfect. Men felt less near to heaven. Their needs were supplied by a heavenly tree called the Household Kalpa Tree, a Tree of Life. It provided garments, ornaments, fruit, and honey so full of a sweet scent, flavor and color that it was highly strengthening. Men lived on this honey not made by bees; but in the course of time, they began to feel a greedy desire to take possession of the Kalpa Trees for themselves. This was a sin and so all these trees were destroyed and all growing things were swallowed up in the earth. The weather changed and it was either too hot or too cold. Humans had to find shelter in caves or build houses, and they nearly died of hunger and thirst. Then did Brahma give men the skill to work with their hands to cultivate the earth and bring forth their own crops.

In this age, the Treta Yuga, lived Manu, the son of Virag. It is said that Manu called into being ten great sages who, in turn, created seven other sages, or Holy Rishis, and with their help Manu taught human beings the sacred laws of Brahma which would lead mankind away from darkness and evil. Yet evil had to increase on earth, so that men might learn the difference between good and evil.

There finally came a time when, led by the demons, the forces of evil captured so many men that goodness in the world lessened by one half. This was the Dwapara Yuga, during which disease and calamity and desire for the things of this world made falsehood overtake truth, and men had to suffer because they sinned.

Manu, whose name means "To Know," yet lived, and often he went alone into the forest, staying there for long periods of time, turning his thoughts to God, silencing every other thought. One day, as he stood by a stream of water, a fish rose from the stream and asked for his protection from the larger fishes that desired to swallow it, and at the same time promising to reward him. Manu placed the fish in a jar and took care of it until it grew larger. Then he put it in a large tank. The fish outgrew the tank and asked to be taken to the river. After some time the fish spoke again to Manu saying that it had grown too large for the river, so Manu carried it to the ocean.

Then the fish smiled and said, "Know thou, O worshipful one, my protector, that the destruction of the world is at hand. The time is here for the evil to be taken from the face of the earth. I will therefore tell thee what thou shouldst do so that thou will be saved. Build a strong and massive ark and furnish it with a long rope. Then enter it with the Seven Rishis and take with thee all the different seeds that grow in the earth and preserve them carefully.

"The many-colored and brilliant clouds will collect in the sky, looking like herds of elephants decked with wreathes of lightning. Suddenly they will burst asunder, and rain will fall without stopping for twelve years until the whole world is covered with water.

"Then the clouds will vanish. The Self-created Lord, the First Cause of everything, will breathe in the winds and go to sleep. The Earth will become covered with water. Without mine aid thou canst not save thyself from this terrible deluge."

It then happened as the fish had said. Manu did as he was advised and set sail on the surging sea with the Seven Rishis and the seeds which he had gathered. He thought of the fish and it arose out of the waters like an island, in the guise of a horned animal. Manu made a noose with the rope and cast it over the animal's horns, and the fish towed the ark over the roaring sea. Tossed by the billows, the vessel reeled about as if it would tip over. No land was in sight. There was water everywhere and none but Manu, the Seven Rishis and the fish could be seen.

After many long years the vessel was towed to the highest peak of the Himavat, which is still called Naubandhana (the harbor), and it was made fast there. The fish then spoke and said, "I am Brahma, the Lord of all creatures. There is none greater than I who saved you from the cataclysm. Manu will create again all beings. By practicing severe austerities will he acquire this power."

Then the fish was seen no more. As the waters sank, Manu descended the mountain, offering to the waters what food he had with him: butter, sour milk, curds and whey. The food became solid and from it rose a woman who said she was his daughter. After that many people were reborn on earth and Manu and the Seven Rishis taught them the laws of Brahma.

According to the scriptures, we live in the fourth great age of man's life on earth, the Kali Yuga. Only one fourth of the original goodness is left. Men turn more and more to wickedness, and the world suffers great troubles, even though there have been men pointing the way to shut off evil from the world.

The Laws of Manu

"The whole Veda is the first source of the sacred law; whatever law has been ordained for any person by Manu, that has been fully declared in the Veda." In this wise was mankind divided into four castes: Brahman, Kshatriya, Vaisya and Sudra.

As the Brahmans sprang from the mouth of Brahma, they are the first-born; they possess the Veda and are by right the lords of this whole creation. The very birth of the Brahmans is an eternal incarnation of the sacred law, for they are born to fulfill the sacred law and become one with Brahma. Whatever exists in the world becomes the property of the Brahmans on account of the excellence of their origin. They are the priests and the teachers. A learned Brahman must carefully study the laws of Manu and instruct his pupils in them. Nobody else shall do it.

Born from the arms of Brahma, the Kshatriyas are born to protect the people; they are the warriors and the guards. The Vaisyas, arising from Brahma's thighs, are the businessmen and skilled traders; they tend cattle, cultivate the land, carry on trade, and lend money. From the feet of Brahma came forth the Sudras, the laboring class, and it is their role to meekly serve the other castes.

Four steps in life are set forth by the laws of Manu: Initiation, Studentship, Householdership and Hermitship.

In the old days, as soon as a boy of any of the three higher castes reached a certain age, he went through an Initiation which enlightened him as to the aim of his life on earth. He then received the knowledge that, although at birth he had entered a world of darkness and unreality, he could live his life in such a way as to make certain his return to the divine and real world of Brahma where he would again find that light which cannot be darkened by shadows and the bliss that can never be disturbed by pleasure or pain.

After his Initiation, the boy selected a teacher. To him his teacher was the image of Brahma and deserved the utmost reverence. As a student, the boy first learned certain rules of conduct: "Let him not answer nor converse with his Guru by reclining on a bed, nor sitting, nor eating, nor speaking with an averted face. Let him do it standing when the Guru is seated. Within the sight of his teacher, the student shall not sit carelessly at ease. Let him not pronounce the mere name of his Guru, even behind his back, without adding an honorific title, and let him not mimic his gait, speech or deportment. Wherever people justly censure or falsely defame a teacher, there the student must cover his ears or depart thence to another place." After learning how to purify himself, to perform the fire worship and the twilight devotions, the student was ready to study the Veda and would stay with his Guru until this was completed.

Having completed his Studentship, the young man could marry, but only a young woman of his own caste. Throughout his married life, the sacrificial fire that had been lighted at his wedding was kept burning. His duties as a Householder included the daily study of the Veda, daily burnt offerings at the fire to all the beings in the world and to the gods, and the giving of gifts to the poor, to the sick, and to animals.

When a man had fulfilled his life as a Householder and when his children were grown up, he left his house and went to live as a Hermit in the forest. Dressed in bark and eating roots, wild fruit and berries, he lived in a cave or at the roots of a tree. He carried the household fire with him and continued making sacrifices to the gods. He meditated on the Veda, cared less and less for his bodily comfort, and prepared himself for death, so that after death he would be able to take the straightest path to Brahma, his Creator.

The Story of Rama

Valmiki was a hermit of the woods. To him there came a Rishi who told him the story of Rama. One day after that, Valmiki went to the river to bathe and came upon two herons playing together on the river bank. Suddenly, a passing hunter shot the male bird, which at once fell dead in a pool of blood. Great was the grief of the female, and Valmiki's heart was so moved by her cries of distress that he began to speak out what he felt in a wonderful meter. So musical and poetic was his speech that the god Brahma approached him and commanded him to compose the story he had heard from the Rishi in this meter. So, Valmiki obeyed Brahma, sat upon a grass carpet, sipped holy water, and became absorbed in thought until visions of the story were revealed before his eyes. Then, verse by verse, he sang the Ramayana; and as long as mountains endure and rivers run toward the sea, so long will the Ramayana (the story of Rama) be repeated by the lips of mankind.

In Lanka (Sri Lanka), Rahvana, King of Demons, had his dwelling. He had grown in power until he was mightier than Yama, the god of death; than Agni, the god of fire; than Vayu, the wind god; and even mightier than Surya, the sun god. Now Rahvana was troubling Indra, the god of thunder. So Indra appealed to Brahma, the creator of the gods, demons and men, to deliver the gods from the clutches of Rahvana. But Brahma was helpless, for he had promised Rahvana at the beginning of all time that he could never be destroyed by mortal men. So Brahma led Indra and the other gods to Vishnu, the preserver, and they prayed Vishnu to save them from the demon king.

Vishnu said, "Be not afraid. Rahvana cannot withstand apes or me. Go therefore, ye gods, toward the earth and take on the bodies of apes; and I will divide myself into four parts and be born as the four sons of Rajah Dasaratha. When I shall battle against Rahvana, you will hasten to my aid."

The Maha Rajah Dasaratha ruled over the ancient kingdom of Ayodhya on the banks of the River Gogra. Ayodhya was a beautiful city of streets, temples, groves and gardens, palaces and ponds of water. Banners flew in the breeze. Brahmans chanted the Vedas, and musicians played music in honor of the Maha Rajah. The walls and towers and gates of the city were all manned with archers and stored with weapons. Brahman Rishis were teaching their pupils in the temples. Kshatriya warriors were training their troops in the use of swords, spears and bows. Vaisyas, the merchants, were selling goods in the marketplaces. Around the city in the fields, the Sudras were cultivating the soil. Men of other castes lower than the Sudras were busy about their trades: jewelers, brass smiths, singing men, dancing women, chariot drivers, flower sellers. Every son from highest to lowest followed in the calling of his father so that there was no confusion.

The Maha Rajah dwelt in his palace in the center of the city and was loved and praised as the greatest Rajah in all the world. He had eight counselors in affairs of state and two Brahmans as his priests and spiritual advisors. He had three queens, and in the course of time they gave him four sons. Rama, the oldest, was the son of Kausalya, the good. Bharata was the son of Kaikeyi, the wicked. The twins, Lakshmana and Satrughna, were the sons of Sumitra, the sweet.

Rama was the most beautiful. The Brahman, Vasishtha, saw in Rama the marks of Vishnu. As a baby he cried for the moon. Not milk, jewels, nor prayers would stop his crying; but when a mirror which reflected the moon was placed in his hand, he thought he had been given the moon and became quiet. As he grew up with his brothers, he rose high above them, like a flag which flutters above a high dome, in all that he learned: grammar, music, painting, dancing, the use of bows and spears, riding horses and elephants, and driving chariots.

When Rama was sixteen, the Rajah of a neighboring kingdom proclaimed that he would give his daughter in marriage to the Kshatriya who could bend the bow of Shiva, a great bow never before bent or strung. Rama and Lakshmana went to the Rajah's court and the bow was brought before them on an eight-wheeled iron chariot. With a smile, Rama lifted the bow, strung it, and bent it with such strength that it snapped in two with a terrible noise like thunder. The earth shook, the mountains echoed as if struck by one of Indra's thunderbolts, and all fell to earth stunned, except for Janaka, the Rajah, Rama and Lakshmana. Thus Rama won Sita, a most beautiful, young woman, as his bride. Great was the rejoicing in the kingdom of Dasaratha.

As the Rajah Dasaratha was getting old, his counselors wanted Rama to be installed as the Young, or Yuvarajah, to take over the rule of the kingdom so that Dasaratha could spend his last years preparing for his death. All the sages and warrior chiefs agreed. Dasaratha, who loved Rama, was overjoyed, and it was proclaimed. Great celebrations were prepared overnight. The city was lit with torches. Bands of music played in the streets. The golden throne was set up under the royal umbrella. Temples were hung with garlands. The roads were watered and covered with carpets of flower petals. From all the countryside people flocked to the city to take part in the celebration.

Kaikeyi, the mother of Bharata, was persuaded by an evil servant woman who hated Rama that if Rama became the Rajah, she and her son would become his slaves. Once long ago Kaikeyi had saved the life of Dasaratha, and he had promised her that if ever she asked, he would grant her two favors. Now Kaikeyi, threatening to poison herself, asked for these favors. One was that Bharata should become the Yuvarajah, and the other was that Rama be sent to the forest for fourteen years. With great sorrow Dasaratha had to keep his promise.

Rama was called before the throne and was told his fate by Kaikeyi. He showed no dismay, gave his father his promise to bide in the forest, and returned to Sita to bid her farewell; but Sita and Lakshmana insisted on going with him. All three walked to the palace in bare feet to bid Dasaratha farewell while the people wept and cried. As the three left the city, many tried to follow Rama, but by the next morning, he had left them behind and entered the frontier of the kingdom whence they had been carried by chariot. So Rama and his companions, Sita and Lakshmana, wandered south toward the River Ganges.

Dasaratha died and Bharata was summoned to take the throne. He asked for Rama, and for the first time he heard the story of his mother's wile. Bharata vowed never to sit in Rama's throne and set out with a large army in search of him. When he found Rama, he begged him to return to Ayodhya. Rama would not break his promise to stay away for fourteen years. Bharata offered to stay instead and let Rama return to rule, but still Rama refused. Then Bharata asked Rama to put on a pair of golden sandals. Rama did so, but then returned them to Bharata, who sadly returned to Ayodhya with Rama's sandals. Then Bharata dressed himself in bark and dwelt outside the city in a jungle, and he placed Rama's sandals there under the royal umbrella as a sign that Rama ruled and that he, Bharata, was guarding the kingdom until Rama's return. There, Bharata stayed throughout the fourteen years that Rama was banished.

In the meantime, Rama, Sita, and Lakshmana wandered through India, crossed the Vindhya Mountains, and built a hut near the mouth of the Godavari River. Thirteen and a half years passed in love, peace, and quiet.

One day, Surpanakha, the sister of the demon Rahvana, wandered up to the hermitage. Seeing Rama, she fell in love with him. She changed herself from an ugly demon into a beautiful maiden; she told him who she was and that she had chosen him for her husband. Rama refused her offer and suggested she marry Lakshmana, who made fun of her, so she sprang at Sita. Rama thrust her back and Lakshmana cut off her ears and nose so that she fled away, wailing like a storm wind. She fled to the other demons in the neighborhood and told them what had happened. They went to capture Rama and Lakshmana but were all killed except for the leader who escaped. Surpanakha summoned fourteen thousand more demons, but Rama and Lakshmana slew them all. Then the demon maiden fled to Lanka and told her brother, the demon king Rahvana, what had happened.

Not long after that, a beautiful deer wandered past the hermitage. It was golden with spots of silver and had horns tipped with sapphires and eyes as blue as lotus flowers. Sita begged Rama to catch it for her as a pet. He went after the deer, leaving Lakshmana to guard Sita. After a chase, Rama shot an arrow which pierced the heart of the deer. The demon brother Rahvana sprang out from the body of the deer, crying out in Rama's voice, "Sita, Sita, save me." Sita heard the call and sent Lakshmana to help Rama. While she was alone and unprotected, Rahvana appeared and carried her off to Lanka in his chariot, which sailed through the air like a great bird, drawn by asses with demon heads.

When Rama and Lakshmana returned and found Sita missing, they were filled with anguish. They wandered in search of her through the forested hills, called for her on every mountain and hill, and asked all birds and beasts to tell the brothers if they had seen her pass. They met the king of the vultures who had seen Rahvana carrying Sita toward the south. They met a demon with one eye and long teeth who hungered for human flesh and coiled his long arms around them. They overcame him, slew him, and burned him. From his ashes rose a dancer of the gods who had been under a spell. He told Rama to go to Lanka, but that first he should seek the aid of the king of the apes.

The story of how Hanuman (son of the wind god, Vayu) and Sugriva (son of Surya, the sun god) helped Rama overcome Rahvana and rescue Sita is set forth in the Ramayana:

Hanuman the monkey and Sugriva agreed to be on earth when Vishnu , the preserver and protector, decided in heaven to come to Rama's aid to rescue Sita. When Rama came to the edge of the land and could see the island to which Sita had been kidnapped and could go no further, Hanuman summoned thousands of monkeys who made a bridge for Rama to use to get to the island. Rama found Sita unharmed, protecting herself with her thoughts of her love for Rama. She could not see the evil around her; all she saw was Rama.

Then Rama engaged Rahvana in earnest battle. Filled with arrogance, Rahvana thought that he could never be destroyed by mortal man assumed that he would defeat his opponent easily, as he had done so many times before. The fighting was so ferocious, so intense, that it lifted right off the earth and continued into the stars. Rama pulled one arrow after the other from his quiver: the arrow of hope, the arrow of light, the arrow of courage, the arrow of fortitude. All the arrows failed even to pierce the body of Rahvana. However, when Rama pulled the arrow of truth from his quiver and sent it soaring through the heavens to the heart of Rahvana, the arrow pierced through to the heart of the fiend. Rahvana realized immediately that this was not Rama but Vishnu appearing as Rama. Once Rahvana saw that his heart was pierced, he also realized that he had been a fool to think that evil could ever prevail over goodness.

The gods were so impressed at Rahvana's realization that they honored him with the funeral of a god. With the death of their king, the demons were overcome. Sita was released and her purity confirmed, as she reunited with Rama to the delight of all surrounding them.

Rama's fourteen years of exile were ended and he returned to Ayodhya with Sita. Bharata and Satrughna were still guarding his kingdom, and the golden sandals were awaiting him. Great was the rejoicing throughout the land, for Rama at last became the Maha Rajah, ruling wisely and well for the rest of his life.

Gautama Buddha 563–483 BC

Once upon a time a householder came forth in the morning after his bath and bowed himself to earth, to Heaven, to the north, south, east and west while he threw rice, red and white, from both his hands. There came a man, with a shining face, dressed in a yellow robe, who saw the householder and asked, "Wherefore bowest thou, brother?"

The householder answered, "Great sir, it is the way our fathers have taught us, at every dawn before our work begins, to hold off evil from the sky above and the earth beneath and from all the winds that blow."

Then spake the shining one,

Scatter not rice but instead offer loving thoughts to all –
To parents as in the East, where rises light –
To teachers as in the South, whence rich gifts come –
To wife and children as in the West, where colors of
*   love and calm gleam as days are done –*
To friends and relations and all men as in the North –
To humblest living things beneath –
To Saints and Angels and the blessed Dead above –
So shall all evil be shut off and so the six main quarters safely kept.

Who was this man with shining face and yellow robe who told the householder to send out loving thoughts and deeds in all directions, instead of rice? He was born in India in 563 BC. I will tell you his story:

King Suddhodana's kingdom lay under the shadow of the Himalaya Mountains. He was rich, just and powerful, but his wife, Queen Maya, had given him no son.

Below the highest heaven, four ruling angels sit and under them is a realm nearer to earth where gather the saintliest spirits who wish to be born on earth. The Lord Buddha was one such saint who waited there. The four angels saw five signs on him that meant that he would soon go to the earth. "Buddha will go again to help the world!" they said.

And he answered, "Yea! Now I go to help the world for the last of many times. After this life which I now seek, I will not need to go into the world again."

That night Queen Maya dreamed that a six-pointed star shot through the heavens, shone into her, and entered her right side. She awoke with a feeling of highest bliss. Though it was yet night, a lovely light shone over half the earth, the hills were shaking, the seas became calm, and all the flowers which only bloom by day opened their blossoms. When she told her dream to the King's dream-readers, they said, "It is a good dream. The Queen shall have a son, a holy child of wondrous wisdom, who shall, if he chooses, free men from ignorance or, if he chooses, shall rule the world."

It came to pass as the dream-readers had said it would. On the day of the child's birth, Queen Maya stood in the Palace Garden under a phalsa tree, tall and straight as a temple tower, with its glossy leaves and flowering blossoms. Knowing the time had come—for all things knew—the tree bent down its boughs to shelter her. The earth put forth a thousand sudden flowers to spread a carpet, while a nearby rock let forth a clear stream of water for the child's first bath. Thus was he born. The news was carried to the Palace, and a bright palanquin came to carry the little Prince home. It was borne by the four angels disguised as servants of the King. And other gods came unto the earth and walked with men that day, though men knew it not, for all of Heaven was glad for the earth's sake, knowing that the Lord Buddha had been born again.

King Suddhodana ordered great celebrations for his son's birth. From all over the kingdom people came to greet their Prince with joy. Among them came a gray-haired Rishi who, in his forest hermitage, had heard the angels singing songs at Buddha's birth. The King and Queen sought to lay their child at the feet of this holy man, but he cried out against it, saying, "Not so! O Babe, I worship thee, for thou art He, the Buddha, who will preach the Law of Wisdom and Love. Alas, I shall never hear it as I will die too soon; but I have at least seen thee!" Then the Rishi told the King that when his son would see four signs—old age, sickness, death and a hermit—he would want to give up his kingdom on earth for a heavenly kingdom.

The Prince was named Siddartha Gautama. When he was eight years old, his father procured a Brahman as his teacher. Soon the Brahman found out that the Prince knew more than his teacher did. Yet the pupil was humble and obedient, gentle and soft-mannered. The boy was an excellent horseman and made a good chariot driver, and he showed greater skill than his playmates in all games.

One spring day, his father took him out to see the countryside where men were busy plowing the fields and sowing grain, where birds flew and sang in the woods, where the thickets were rustling with lizards and beetles and ants and other creeping things pleased at the springtime. All things seemed busy and happy, and Prince Siddartha rejoiced. But when he looked deeper, he saw how hard the plowmen had to work so that the sweat dropped from their brows. He saw the goads, with nails at the ends, which they pricked into their oxen's flanks to make them go. He saw how the lizards fed on the ants, and how the birds ate the butterflies. He saw life living upon death. The Prince sighed and said to his father, "Is this the happy world you brought me out to see?"

Then he left his father and sat beneath a rose-apple tree and turned his mind to what he had seen. So great was the pity that filled him, so great the longing to help all suffering beings, that five holy angels, who were flying high over the rose-apple tree felt the divine force and sacred presence of a pure being and stopped in their flight. They heard a voice crying, "This is He who shall help the world. Descend and worship him." So the bright ones came, folded their wings before him, and sang a song of praise. In the late afternoon the Prince was still sitting under the tree when the servants of the King came in search of him. The sun was setting, and all the shadows had moved except those of the rose-apple, whose shade stayed so long as the Prince sat there. The King's servants heard a voice from the blossoms of the tree say, "Let the King's son be. Till the shadow goes from his heart, my shade will not shift."

As Siddartha grew older, his father looked forward to the day when the Prince would become King. When he saw this thoughtful sadness in the boy, he feared what the Rishi had said at his birth, that when Siddartha saw old age, sickness, death and a hermit who had withdrawn from life, he would forsake the throne.

The King surrounded his son with delights; he built him three palaces amidst fair gardens and groves where the Prince could wander. Yet the Prince was thoughtful and sad at times. The King consulted his advisors who suggested that Siddartha should have a wife. This soon was brought to pass when the Prince met and fell in love with beautiful Yasodhara. He had to win her at a *swayamwara* where many other princes also strove. He bent a bow which none could bend and shot an arrow further than any. He cut through two trees with a sword stroke so neatly that the cut could not be seen, until the angels of the air blew light breaths from the south and the two green crowns crashed in the sand. He tamed and rode a wild horse which no one else could handle.

After Siddartha's marriage, the King built a pleasure palace for him and his bride. It was enclosed by a high wall and guarded gates. Within no one was allowed to be old, sad or sick. No one was allowed to mention old age, sorrow, sickness or death. Here the Prince and Princess lived in greatest comfort amid beautiful things and sights and sounds, and in this way the King hoped to win Siddartha's heart for his kingdom.

One day Siddartha asked to be taken out in his chariot, beyond the walls, to see that land and those people he would rule. The King agreed but sent out criers to tell all people that no unhappy sights must greet their prince; no sick, old, blind or crippled people must be out on the roads or streets. And although the people swept and garlanded their city for the Prince's visit, yet did the Prince come upon an old and wrinkled man dressed in rags. His back was bent, his eyes were red with weeping, his mouth toothless. In one skinny hand he held a staff to hold him up on his bony legs. The other hand was pressed to his side. His breath came in painful gasps as he cried out, "Alms, good people, give me alms, for tomorrow I die!"

Then he coughed and choked, and the people thrust him out of the Prince's way, shouting, "The Prince! Can't you see? Get out of his sight."

Never having been allowed to see an old person, Siddartha turned to his charioteer and exclaimed, "What is this thing that looks like a man, yet seems so bowed and miserable, so horrible, so sad? Are men born like this sometimes? What does it mean when he says, 'Tomorrow I shall die'?"

The charioteer whispered, "This, my Prince, is the way of life. Once this old man was as young as you, straight and strong, but now his youth is gone."

No sooner had the Prince suffered this shock than he saw a beggar covered with the awful spots of a deadly disease. The charioteer said, "That too is the way of life."

Then there appeared a group of wailing people who were chanting, "Rama, Rama, hear us!" Upon a bamboo stretcher they were carrying one who lay stiff and cold, one who was dead. "This," said the charioteer, "is the end of life."

Siddartha turned homeward with tears in his eyes and a great pity in his heart, saying, "I have always thought it lovely to live, but now I see that life is not what I thought. How can Brahma make a world and allow such misery within it? If he is all powerful and leaves the world so, then he is not good. But if he is not powerful to change it, then he is not God."

That night Yasodhara had three dreams. The first was of a great white bull, wearing a jewel of great worth upon his forehead and walking through the city streets towards the gates. A voice called, "If you let him leave the city, all the city's glory will go with him." But none could stop him. She clasped his neck and tried, but he tossed her aside and went out.

In the second dream, the four ruling angels with all their retinue swept into the city, and the golden flag of Indra, which flew on the gate, fluttered and fell. A new one of silver, covered with rubies, rose in its place. From the new flag fell wonderful words which brought peace to all who heard them. Then she dreamed that she could not find Siddartha no matter where she searched, and a voice cried out, "The time is come."

She awoke and told Siddartha her dreams. He comforted her and she slept again, but he had heard the words, "The time is come" in his own heart, and he rose from the bed. For now he had decided that so long as sorrow, sickness and death existed in the world, he would go in search of a way to understand them, to find an answer to his question of why Brahma had made such a world.

He left his wife in the night and went forth in his chariot, riding till dawn. Then he stepped down, gave his royal robes and jewels to the charioteer, cut his long hair off with his sword and sent all back to the King with this message: "Siddartha prays the King that he will forget him until he comes back having won wisdom from his lonely searchings."

Along the way he went, he came upon some hermits who believed that if they tortured their bodies, they would find their souls and so reach Brahma, or Truth. Some stood day and night with lifted arms until the arms withered and stiffened. Others clenched their hands for so long that their nails grew through their suffering palms. Some walked on sandals lined with nails or drove thorns into their flesh. The Prince did not see how this was good, for they were but adding pain to a world already too full of it. So he left their company.

He met a herdsman taking lambs to a sacrifice at a king's palace. Siddartha went with him, but when he arrived and saw the sacrificial fire and the ceremonies of preparation for the slaughtering of the lambs, he told the king and his priests that life is something all can take but none can give; that all creatures love and try to keep life wonderful, dear and pleasant to each, however small; and that mankind who prays for mercy from the gods shows here no mercy to the animals who look to him as to a god. So truly spoken, so gently spoken were his words that the king ordered all sacrifices stopped, in fact all slaughter of animals. This king tried to persuade Siddartha to stay with him to teach him and his people his wisdom and to rule his kingdom at his death. Siddartha answered that he had already had such a kingdom and now looked for something greater.

At length he journeyed up into the mountains until he came to a place where a great tree, the Bodhi-Tree, stood. Here, it was foretold, would the truth be revealed to him. With slow pace, he went to the tree. Now all the world rejoiced. As he sat down under the tree, the grass bowed to worship him, flowers sprang up around his feet, the forest boughs bent down to shade him, and cool breezes came to fan him. Wild animals came to gaze at him, panther and deer standing at peace side by side. The cobra opened its hood to honor him, and butterflies flew about his head. Then Siddartha vowed never to leave the place until he had discovered the truth.

Night came on, bringing Mara, the Evil One, who came to tempt Siddartha with the seven deadly sins: the Sin of Self, "Why think of other people?"; the Sin of Doubt, "How do you know that what you do is right?"; on and on with many others. Siddartha sat serenely and dismissed each temptation, one by one.

The earth became still, and the Prince saw a Light in which were revealed his five hundred and fifty past lives on earth. He saw that each good life led to more good, each evil life to more evil.

In the next vision he saw into all the worlds that lie beyond the earth and saw those things which had happened, age after age. At length he felt the Power which builds the worlds, unbuilds, and builds again, and rules all things according to the rule of virtue: beauty, truth and use, so that all do well who serve this Power and do ill who hinder It.

In the next watch he saw how Sorrow moves wherever life is because men think that what they see and hear with physical sight and hearing is real even though it always comes to an end. He saw that men must live again and again until they find that which does not come to an end. When they find that, they can enter Nirvana where nothing changes because it is everlasting. Then are men freed from the wheel of repeated lives on earth.

As this truth entered Siddartha's soul, he took on his heavenly name, Buddha. The sun rose and all the world felt holy. Men felt peaceful as they woke from sleep, sick men leapt laughing from beds of pain, the dying smiled with joy, and far away Yasodhara's sad heart felt sudden bliss.

Ancient Persia

O maker of the material world,
O thou holy one,
Which are the places
Where the earth feels most happy?

It is the place whereon
One of the faithful erects a house
With a priest within,
With cattle,
With a wife, with children,
And good herds within –

It is the place where
One of the faithful tends
Most corn, grass and fruit,
Where he waters the ground
That is dry,
Or drains ground that is too wet.

It is the place where
There is most increase
Of flocks and herds.

It is the place where
Flocks and herds yield
Most dung.

In ancient Persia
men knew that
the physical world
was not
the everlasting world,
but they were to work
on the earth
to transform it
and bring it closer
to the real world.

The Powers of Light and the Powers of Darkness

Zrvan Akaran, that single Power, produced the Divine Light. From this Light sprang the First-born, Ahura Mazda, who created the pure world, the ranks of angels, and a light which was a reflection of the Divine Light.

The second-born, Ahriman, was hungry for power and sought to take it from Ahura Mazda. For this he was banished to realms of darkness and night. There he created the Daêvas, demons to help him shatter the power of Life which Ahura Mazda had placed in the light.

From the scattered bits of life, Ahura Mazda fashioned the first man and the first woman; but Ahriman tempted the woman with fruit and milk so that in eating it she sinned against Ahura Mazda. Thus began the war between good and evil.

Ahura Mazda created sixteen perfect lands, and against them Ahriman brought winter with its ice and snow, whirlwinds, floods, serpents and vermin. Ahriman fought against goodness, justice, patience, pity and peace. Ahura Mazda had a weapon which he knew could never be conquered by evil: "the good and righteous human being who thinks good thoughts, speaks good words and does good deeds," and who works upon the world to lift it out of darkness toward the light.

Jemshid was such a man. He received "the law" from Ahura Mazda but he refused to be a teacher of mankind. Instead he offered to make all beings on earth increase and grow.

Ahura Mazda gave Jemshid a golden seal and a golden dagger. His body shining with light, Jemshid turned southward toward the sun, pressed the golden seal into the earth, then plowed the earth with the golden dagger, saying, "O Spirit of Earth, kindly open and increase, to bear flocks and herds and men." The earth responded and the numbers of flocks and herds, dogs and birds and men increased until there was no room for any more.

Ahura Mazda warned Jemshid that an evil winter fathered by Ahriman was to come, and he instructed Jemshid to build a *Vara* (shelter) two miles square with high walls. In the Vara were to be water tanks, houses, fires, and some of every kind of plant, of animal, and of human being.

And so it came to pass. The evil winter descended upon the earth and only those within the Vara lived on. Then the deep snows melted, and there was a flood that covered the world. Those to whom Jemshid had given shelter were saved, and they fathered a new race.

The struggle between Ahura Mazda and Ahriman continued unceasingly. Ahura Mazda won people to live in peace while Ahriman filled others with evil wishes and warlike feelings that sought to end all peaceful ways of life.

Ahura Mazda's people prayed for help, and Ahura Mazda sent one to earth who would save his people from Ahriman. This savior was Zarathustra. He came to earth after Jemshid's rule was ended.

Zarathustra

At Zarathustra's birth all nature rejoiced. The trees, the rivers and the mountains sang songs of joy for the victory of God over the Devil. A Divine Light illuminated the world, and as the child came forth into the Light, he laughed aloud.

Evil spirits tried to bring about the baby's death. One tried to twist off his head as he lay in the cradle, but its hand withered as it reached out. Another threw the child in the way of a herd of cattle, but one ox, guided by the hand of Ahura Mazda, stood guard over him and saved him from being trampled to death. A third demon imprisoned the child in a den of wolves, but the wolves refused to harm him and brought in a mother sheep to give the child milk.

As a young man, Zarathustra went about among the people, helping the old, healing the sick, feeding the hungry, comforting the sorrowing, lightening the loads of beasts of burden. (Somewhere it has been said that Manu from India was his teacher.)

When he was thirty years old, Zarathustra was meditating in a cave, and all of a sudden he beheld Ahura Mazda face to face, and Ahura Mazda allowed him to enter Heaven and learn the secrets of the world: the difference between the truth and the lie, between the light and the darkness. Then Zarathustra returned to his fellow men to teach them what he had learned. These teachings are in the *Avesta*, the sacred book of the Persians.

Zarathustra was not only the first Teacher of his people, but he was also called the first Priest and the first Plowman. As a Priest he taught the Persians of the glory of the Light which shines in the sun, the glory of Ahura Mazda. As a Plowman he taught the people how to plow the earth and make broad fields and to water them by channeling streams from the melting snows of the hills. He taught them to sow seed and tend plants, to ennoble wild trees so that they brought forth sweet fruit such as plums, pears and apples. He also taught men how to tame wild animals so that they served the righteous man.

Ahriman's spirits tried to overcome Zarathustra at every turn, but the young man succeeded in overcoming them until his mission on earth had been accomplished. When he died, Zarathustra was at worship in the Temple of the Sacred Fire which had been laid to ruins by attacking armies. At the moment of his last breath, a rainbow appeared over the sky above the Temple.

Zarathustra had once asked Ahura Mazda, "What is the rainbow?" And Ahura Mazda had answered, "The rainbow is the smile of the souls in heaven giving courage to the sorrowing souls on earth."

SOME OF ZARATHUSTRA'S TEACHINGS

All that which is good comes from Ahura Mazda, the being who lives in the light behind the light of the sun. The world is created by the light and lives in it, but darkness also entered the physical world. All is in struggle between the forces of light and of darkness, between Ahura Mazda and Ahriman.

Unhappy is the land that has lain unsown and wants a good husbandman. To him who tills the earth, the earth says, "O thou man, who dost till me with the left arm and the right, to thee shall I bring forth all manner of food; to thee shall I first bring corn."

No one who does not eat has strength to do works of holiness, to do works of husbandry, or to have children. By eating, every material creature lives. By not eating it dies away.

Ahura Mazda brings healing plants. Many hundreds, thousands, myriads grow up to help man withstand sickness, fever, and infection which Ahriman has created against mortals. Ten thousand healing plants he brought down from heaven to grow up around the tree of eternal life.

⸻

When the sun, the Light, dawns each morning, it is time for people to get up, to pray to the Light, and to do their work in the light of day. But a demon of laziness tries to put people back to sleep again. The cock crows to drive away the demon. No demon can enter a house where there is a cock. At the sound of his crowing, the demons are dazzled and flee away.

⸻

No house could subsist on earth but for the house-dog and the shepherd dog who watch against the thief and the wolf, Ahriman's servants. If a man strikes or hurts a house-dog or a shepherd dog, it will be his punishment that, when he dies, no soul will come to meet him and help him in the other world.

⸻

A MORNING AND EVENING PRAYER

All good thoughts, all good words, all good deeds I do willingly.
All evil thoughts, all evil words, all evil deeds I do unwillingly.
All good thoughts, all good words, all good deeds will reach Paradise.
All evil thoughts, all evil words, all evil deeds will reach Hell.
And all good thoughts, all good words, all good deeds are the badge
    of the righteous for Paradise.

Mesopotamia

URUK-OF-THE-WALLS

Behold, is it not the noblest of cities?
Observe the walls
If they be not made
All of fired bricks!
Inspect them,
How they are molded together.
Look out over the extent of the city,
See how it is arranged,
One third being houses and dwellings,
One third groves of trees,
And one third the precinct of the temples!

THE LAND OF NO RETURN

The house of darkness,
The house men enter
But cannot depart from,
The road men go
But cannot return,
The house from whose dwellers
The light is withdrawn,
The place where dust is their food,
Their nourishment clay.
The light they behold not,
In darkness they dwell.
They are clothed like birds,
All fluttering wings.
On the door and the gateposts
The dust lieth deep!

THE MEASURE OF THE SUN'S COURSE

Look at a man who goes about
Not as a greybeard,
And not as a child,
Who neither runs too swiftly
Nor walks too slowly –
And you will behold
The measure of the sun's course.

∼

It was the great mission of the Babylonians
to draw forth from the laws of measure
prevailing in the heavens everything that
must be incorporated into civilization
for the needs of outer, practical life.
At the same time it was their mission
to relate everything to the human being.

Gilgamesh

Gilgamesh was a king and the descendant of a king, born in the royal palace at Uruk on the east bank of the Euphrates River, one hundred miles from the sea and near to Ur of the Chaldees in the land of Sumeria. He lived between 2800 and 2500 BC. Many years later in about 2100 BC, a great poem was written about him. It tells that Gilgamesh was two-thirds god and one-third man. He was a great hunter of lions and wild bulls. No one could match his strength. No one dared challenge him in wrestling.

He swaggered through the streets of his city, hunted, and boasted until the elders of the city could stand it no more and they beseeched Aruru, the goddess of their city, "Make another man to match him!" They made many sacrifices to Aruru, and she was pleased and took pity on them. She descended from her golden couch and, reaching the river, gathered clay and shaped a man with the thighs and long tail of a bull, but from the waist up his shape was that of a man. He came to life as a south wind blew and brought him breath. He became Eabani or Enkidu. Free as a breeze and happy as a young colt, Enkidu bounded from the river. He was filled with daring and was swift of foot.

The people of Uruk admired him so much that Gilgamesh determined to capture Enkidu, especially when it became known that Enkidu gave his protection to the animals Gilgamesh hunted. Saving them from the hunter's traps, Enkidu guided them to safe places in the desert.

At sunset Gilgamesh sent his bravest hunter to the desert watering hole where Enkidu usually led his animal flocks to drink. With the hunter went a woman of the palace. She had such beauty that she lured Enkidu away from the animals and told him of the beauty of Uruk, its comforts, and the delights of the company of other men. Enkidu fell in love with the woman, went with her, and took up life as a man in the palace.

Not long after this, Gilgamesh had a terrible nightmare that frightened him even after he awoke. It was of a great warrior who came from the stars to wrestle with him and who conquered him. When he told Ninmah, his mother, of his dream, she comforted him, saying that he would indeed wrestle with this stranger, but that good would come of it.

One night Gilgamesh held a party and led a band of merry, young men from house to house, wherever they could find drink and entertainment. Enkidu was of this band, and when Gilgamesh sought to enter one of these houses, Enkidu barred his way. Expecting to fell him, Gilgamesh aimed a blow at Enkidu's face, but instead Enkidu grasped the shoulders of Gilgamesh and wrestled with him. It was the first time in his life that Gilgamesh had ever felt a strength equal to his own. As they wrestled, neither one could budge the other.

At length Gilgamesh loosened his hold, stepped back and laughed, all his anger gone. From that time on Gilgamesh and Enkidu were inseparable friends all the days of their lives. Enkidu was always at the side of the King, and the King no longer swaggered and boasted of his strength. He lost his old, evil habits, and the people of Uruk were pleased.

However, amid the comforts of the luxurious palace, Enkidu was unhappy. He longed for the wild places where he had spent his youth. One night he, too, had a terrifying dream. In his dream, Enkidu saw a black monster that swooped down upon him and carried him into the underworld realm of Nergal, king of darkness. There, in great heaps, lay those who had died, and Enkidu could see that their only food was mud.

When told of this dream, Gilgamesh summoned dream interpreters to read its meaning. They advised that Gilgamesh and Enkidu must make a sacrifice to the sun god, Shamash. During the sacrificial rites, the god spoke to the priests and to Gilgamesh, telling him he must leave Uruk and journey to the Cedar Mountain which was guarded by the monster Humbaba. Once there, he must kill the monster and deliver all the land from evil.

Armed with flashing daggers and war clubs, Gilgamesh and Enkidu set out on their great adventure. If Gilgamesh had been alone, he would have dreaded to meet the monster Humbaba, but with Enkidu by his side, he did not fear.

For weeks and weeks they walked through a land that looked as vast as the ocean. The rolling hills stretched yellow and treeless. Only the hawk and the eagle soared overhead. Over all the desert lay a yellowish haze, through which the flying clouds cast shadows that stood like black pillars holding up the sky.

Finally, over the crest of a hill, they saw the magnificent Cedar Mountain. Long before an ancient god had made Humbaba guardian of its great, dark green trees. With delight the two heroes greeted the shade of the scented trees. They followed a path to the top of the mountain and found there a stockade of seven magic trees which surrounded the domain of Humbaba.

Suddenly terrified, Enkidu begged Gilgamesh not to seek out the monster as darkness was falling, but Gilgamesh would not wait. He called out in a loud voice, ordering Humbaba to appear and meet them in battle. There was only silence and the sound of the wind in the trees. Wrapping themselves in their robes, the two of them slept.

Toward morning Enkidu awoke to find Gilgamesh leaning over him to say, "I have dreamed that, lo, the earth shook and the heavens rained fire! All around me death fell from the clouds."

As Enkidu assured Gilgamesh that the dream surely predicted that they would destroy Humbaba, they prepared for battle. Humbaba breathed forth the wind of his breath, and all the way down the mountainside, the lofty cedars bowed their heads to the tempest. Gilgamesh and Enkidu hardly had time to draw their daggers before Humbaba, roaring and shrieking with the winds, charged toward them.

Back and forth the battle raged between Gilgamesh and Humbaba. Gilgamesh felt his strength well up within him as he swung his war club to finally hurl down the monster so that Enkidu could rush upon him and cut off his head. Thus, together, they fulfilled the task that had been set for them by Shamash: to rid the world of such an evil one.

After the battle the warriors cleansed themselves, put on fresh garments, and made offerings to the gods. It was then that Ishtar, the goddess of love, appeared before Gilgamesh to congratulate him on his victory.

Gilgamesh looked so handsome in his gold helmet and white tunic that Ishtar tried to lure him into love for her. He answered her with some anger, "I know what you have done to those who have loved you, Ishtar! The stallion who worshiped you was condemned to pull the heavy war chariot, the shepherds of the hills who were charmed by you were changed into leopards that ate the little lambs. And the youth Tammuz, who loved you, you sent to the house of the dead so that every year after the harvest, the snows of winter steal down the river valleys and cover our land with ice."

Thus did Gilgamesh spurn Ishtar, and she soon took her revenge. She persuaded her father Anu to send the Bull of Heaven to destroy the city of Uruk. But Enkidu, in combat, overcame the bull.

Soon after that Enkidu became ill, cursed by Ishtar. His sickness lasted for twelve days, and on the thirteenth day he died in the arms of his friend.

Unable to bear his grief, Gilgamesh rushed out of the palace like a wild man. He could not be comforted, for as he pictured Enkidu in the House of Death, with mud as his only food, he knew that he, too, would die some day.

Gilgamesh knew of a man who had received the gift of immortality, Utnapishtim, a holy man of Shurupak, and he made up his mind to seek out this man. Perhaps Utnapishtim would be willing to divulge his secret, and perhaps Gilgamesh would be able to return to Uruk with it, bring Enkidu back to life, and save the whole race of mankind from having to die.

Taking leave of Uruk and his weeping mother and fearless of the dangers of the burning desert, he set out toward the west. The journey was long and hard. His garments were torn off by the thorn bushes, and he had to grapple with lions and use their skins for clothing.

At last he reached the Mountain of the Sun. In its depths there was a dark, cold tunnel through which he would have to pass. It was guarded by men with fiery heads and the tails of scorpions. They stopped Gilgamesh from entering, saying, "Only the sun, in the course of the night, makes this passage. No mortal has ever done so."

"Open your gates!" Gilgamesh roared. "I fear no danger here." And the gates were opened.

For twice eleven hours he walked through the darkness that made him feel as if he were descending into the House of Death. Fear and terror shook his soul. Suddenly he saw a pinpoint of light ahead and ran toward it, out of the dark and into a wondrous garden beside a blue-green sea. Amid pools and flowers stood the holy tree of the gods, the tree of life, covered with all kinds of sweet and fragrant fruits. Its branches were of lapis lazuli flecked with gold. Under it the earth was carpeted with sparkling, precious stones. Here lived the goddess Siduri, who asked him about his woe.

Gilgamesh told her of the death of Enkidu and of his own fear of death. "I seek Utnapishtim who has overcome death. Tell me how I might reach him and learn the secret of immortality."

Siduri answered, "The immortality you crave you will never find, for when the gods created man, death was his portion, and life they held for their own." Yet she told him, "Utnapishtim lives across this sea. But these are the waters of death, and no man except yonder boatman has ever crossed them. Go to him and he may help you."

Thus it was that, instructed by the boatman, Gilgamesh crossed the sea and reached the island of Utnapishtim. He found Utnapishtim sitting on a throne with his wife beside him. When Gilgamesh asked the immortal how he too could obtain eternal life, Utnapishtim answered, "Do you expect a house to last for all time? Does a river stay in flood forever? Nothing is permanent!"

Gilgamesh was not put off. "You, Utnapishtim, have been given everlasting life! Tell me your secret."

Whereupon Utnapishtim answered, "I will reveal it though it is known only to the gods and to myself. Once, long ago, the gods determined to destroy man in a great flood. Had it not been for the warning of Ea, god of the waters, I too would have perished. But through the reeds of my hut, Ea whispered, 'Build a ship, Utnapishtim, and take upon it all living creatures that are yours.'

"I did as I was told and, early one morning, when an awesome cloud appeared, I entered the ship and sealed it up. A blackness, lit only by torches of lightning, fell over the earth. The wind struck, shattering the land like a cup, and then the waters fell, filling the land and, in the end, drowning the mountains. Even the gods were terrified and flew up unto the heaven of Anu, to cringe there like dogs.

"For seven days the flood-winds swept the world, and then there was an end. All living things had died except what I had saved. When I opened a hatch and the light poured down, I bowed low and wept.

"A mountaintop appeared above the waters and my ship drifted onto it. After seven days I released a dove, but it found no resting place, and it returned. I sent forth a swallow, and it too came back. Finally I let loose a raven, and it did not return.

"I led forth my family and animals to the mountaintop and offered a sacrifice of thanksgiving. The gods smelled the sweet odor and swarmed around me. I was led back onto the ship. There the gods bade me kneel with my wife at my side. And then these words were spoken over our heads: 'Before this, Utnapishtim has been mortal. From this time on, Utnapishtim and his wife shall be like gods. Far away shall they dwell, at the mouth of the rivers.'"

As Utnapishtim ended his story, he saw that Gilgamesh, wearied by all his hardships, had fallen asleep. Utnapishtim wakened him, saying, "Don't you know that immortals never sleep, O King Gilgamesh! You can win knowledge of immortality if you can remain awake for six days and seven nights."

Gilgamesh tried to stay awake but soon his head was nodding, his eyelids closed, and he was sound asleep again. Utnapishtim then ordered his wife to bake a fresh loaf of bread for each day that Gilgamesh slept. She baked seven loaves and placed them at his head while he slept.

When Utnapishtim awakened him, Gilgamesh denied that he had slept. "Then count the loaves, O King, a fresh one baked each day that you slumbered."

Gilgamesh counted the loaves. The first was still fresh and warm, but the second was cold. The third was already stale and the fourth hard. The fifth was cracked and dry, the sixth black, and the seventh had begun to mold.

Now Gilgamesh knew that his quest had been in vain. Yet Utnapishtim offered solace and told Gilgamesh that he could restore his friend if he could pluck the flower of life and youth that grew at the bottom of the sea. Gilgamesh did not hesitate. Tying heavy stones on his feet, he sank to the bottom of the sea and found the plant. He picked it, then released the stones, and rose to the surface.

"This is a possession beyond belief!" he cried. "No matter how old, whoever eats of it will become young again. I myself will taste it, but first I will take it to Enkidu and then to Uruk to let the old men regain their lost youth."

Gilgamesh returned across the waters of death and made his way through the desert toward Uruk. As he drew near to his city, weary and dusty, he came to a spring-fed pool and decided to bathe therein. He laid his precious plant on the bank. While he was swimming, a snake smelled the plant, slid over to it and devoured it. Gilgamesh wept. "Now Enkidu will never live, and death, the fate of all men, shall be mine," he mourned.

Mesopotamia

The Greek name for "The Land between the Rivers"

Who were the people whose king was Gilgamesh? They are known as the Sumerians, the earliest inhabitants of Mesopotamia. In the history of Western civilization, writing began with the Sumerians; Sumerian written records are the oldest writings known on earth. The poetry of Enheduanna and the epic of Gilgamesh are among them. Written in clay, other records have also been unearthed in the 20th century. Thousands of hard clay tablets have been found, covered with wedge-shaped marks that, when they were deciphered, revealed the life and history of the people of Sumeria, Babylonia, and Assyria in times long before Christ.

Now called cuneiform, these clay records tell of many things. Some are pages of "books," full of stories and beliefs, stories of heroes, of how the world was made. Some are records about the stars, about medicine, about time-telling. Some are the first written laws. Some are letters from a king to various governors and officers who served under him. Some are histories of wars and conquests. Some are the accounts of transactions of traders. Thus, the history of this time, this land, was discovered from the writings and the sculptures of the people themselves. Many archaeologists and scholars worked for years, digging in mounds, gathering records, learning how to read them, fitting them together, and then translating them for us to read. Many more are still being translated. We owe them our thanks.

Before the time of the Sumerians there had been no writing. All knowledge was handed on by word of mouth, as in the Vedas. The Semites, ancient desert people, were nomads ever in search of pastures for their sheep and goats. They lived without boundaries, without laws and without writing.

Then Sumerians, mountaineers who moved down from the mountains and took possession of the southern part of the Plain of Shinar, built settlements of mud-brick houses to live in, and they built towers called ziggurats or step pyramids out of sun-baked brick so that their mountain gods could dwell there as on a mountaintop. Along the low banks of the Euphrates River, they dug ditches and trenches to let the river water flow over the earth which they tilled for growing barley and wheat. They used oxen for plowing, had wheeled carts, made pans and dishes of copper, and carried on trade.

For about three hundred years, from 3050 BC on, the Sumerian towns were city-kingdoms, each with its temple tower surrounded by the houses of the people and each with its ruler-priest who saw to it that the land around the city was irrigated and that no one from another city-kingdom took possession of it. But the time came when the Semites, led by their warrior chief Sargon, invaded the lands of the Sumerians and conquered them.

Having won all this land, the nomads had to settle down and so, although Sargon conquered the Sumerians with arms, the Sumerians conquered the nomads through their way of life. For now the nomads started living in mud houses instead of tents. They learned to farm, to trade, to do metal work and to write. Thus the two peoples became as one nation. This became the world of Gilgamesh.

The Sumerians gave us the 360 degrees of a circle, the 24-hour day, the 60-minute hour, and the 60-second minute. They understood basic geometry and had a number base of 60, instead of our number base of 10.

A thousand years later, the little town of Babylon, under a king named Hammurabi, became the leading city, and all the land around it was called Babylonia. Like those before him, Hammurabi was a priest-king. An eight-foot shaft of stone, unearthed by archaeologists, shows him receiving laws from the Sun-God. Fifty-five of his letters, on clay tablets to carry commands to the Babylonian officials, reveal events of the time.

The ziggurats (temples) were the centers of life in the towns of Babylonia, as they had been in Sumerian times. The priests (rulers) owned the land, collected and loaned money for business, and had to keep accounts, and so developed a system of numbers. But the order of life they established among people on earth was related to the order they observed in the stars of heaven.

The Babylonians were the first astronomers. Through a strict and exact observation of the stars, sun, and moon and their rhythmic movements, they developed earthly measures of time. The length of a year they derived from the position of the sun at noon on June 21st when it shone directly down upon the main street in Babylon. They observed the sun return to this position every 365 days, and this became the measure of the year. They saw that the moon shifted the position of its rising to return to the original position again every 29 days, and this became the measure of the month. They observed five stars that also shifted their positions and wandered through the sky in regular rhythm. These five "wanderers," or planets, together with the sun and moon, gave them the measure of the week as seven days.

We, of this day and age, still measure the year, the month, and the week as they were measured by the Babylonian priests in the rhythmical movements and numbers of the heavenly lights. When we look up to the starry sky, perhaps we can feel what these priestly astronomers did: that the stars were the outer signs of the god-like powers that lived within them and influenced the lives of men on earth.

In their ziggurats of sun-dried brick, the Babylonians designed an image of heaven and earth. The ziggurat was square for the four corners of the earth. It ascended in seven steps, each step a symbol of the seven heavenly lights: the sun, the moon and the five planets, and at the same time of the seven earthly metals: gold, silver, copper, iron, mercury, tin and lead. The named it "El-temen-an-ki," meaning "The House of the Foundation Stone of Heaven and Earth."

Enheduanna

Long before the epic of Gilgamesh was written, the first literature known in the history of the Western world was being composed by a princess, and her name was Enheduanna. The only daughter of the great Semite king, Sargon, she lived between 2285 and 2250 BC, and she wrote many fiery poems.

King Sargon must have trusted her a great deal because he put her in charge of the southern part of his kingdom, including the city of Ur, where Gilgamesh had once lived, and where Enheduanna eventually settled. King Sargon also made her a high priestess and sent her from city to city in his southern kingdom to visit the temples, which were designed to honor the gods. Enheduanna wrote a special poem for each of these temples to inspire the people to honor their gods and to live good lives.

Enheduanna loved one goddess the most, Inanna, also known as Ishtar. The princess wrote many hymns to Inanna who was not only a storm goddess but who also had many other powers. Enheduanna wrote of her in a long poem called "Lady of Largest Heart." Here are parts of it translated by Betty De Shong Meador:

She is Inanna
Bearer of happiness
whose strapping command
hip-dagger in hand
spreads radiance over the land…

She wears
the carved-out ground plan
of heaven and earth

who seeks her word …
cannot fathom her plan's execution
she holds the life of heaven
with her single hand
fierce lady Wildcat…
you draw men into unending strife
or crown with fame a favored person's life.

Yet, to Enheduanna, Inanna was not only a powerful goddess, who could change men into women and vice versa, but she was also in charge of many other opposites: sickness and health, good and bad business practices, war and peace. Family life, trade and healing were also part of her domain.

To smooth the traveler's road
To clear a path for the weak
Are yours Inanna…

To hand out tender mercies
restore your heart to someone
are yours Inanna

heart trembling weakness
shivering cramps illness
are yours Inanna…

to have a husband to have a wife
to thrive in the goodness of love
are yours Inanna

to spark a quarrel
with love's lusty delight
is yours Inanna

to be negligent
and tend carefully
are yours Inanna

to build a house
construct the women's rooms
furnish them
to kiss a baby's lips
are yours Inanna

to spread the leg stride
to footrace
to win
are yours Inanna

to mingle
the brute the strong
the downtrodden the weak
are yours Inanna…

To joke inflame a quarrel
To defile to esteem
Are yours Inanna…

To be all knowing
is yours Inanna

to build a bird's nest
safe in a sound branch
make indestructible
are yours Inanna…

to gather the scattered
restore the living place
are yours Inanna

Enheduanna goes on is this vein and ends by praising the many moods and capacities of this great goddess: "You alone are sublime/praise your name." Toward the end of the poem, the poetess adds:

I
I am Enheduanna
High priestess of Nanna
With single heart
I am devoted to Nanna.

In another of her poems, "The Exaltation of Inanna," she writes about how a man took away her power and how, with the help of Inanna, she got it back:

That man threw me out of the temple
I who served triumphant

he made me fly
like swallows swept
from their holes in the wall

he eats away at my life
I wander through thorny brush in the mountains
he robbed me
of the true crown
of the High Priestess.

Enheduanna is in despair and feels she is dying. She can no longer pray in the temple to ask Inanna for help, and she can no longer interpret dreams, one of her jobs as High Priestess, so she begs Inanna for help. Eventually she is restored as High Priestess, and the rest of her poem proclaims honor and gratitude to Inanna.

In all, Enheduanna left us 4500 lines of powerful poetry, which was not translated until the end of the 20th century. Written in cuneiform, her brilliant poetry comes before any other known writer of literature. Thus, the first known literary writer is actually woman, Enheduanna.

The Christmas Star

Long before the birth of Christ, wise men of the East had been watchers of the stars. Knowledge of the stars was the highest of all learning, and through it men sought to untangle the threads of the mystery of life, to foretell what would happen on earth.

The days and the nights, the months and the years were measured and marked by the risings and settings of sun, moon and stars. The darkest moment of the year was when the sun rose to its lowest point in the heavens, thus bringing the longest night to earth. The wise men of Chaldea celebrated this time of the year as "the Midnight Hour" and the longest night as the "Night of Consecration."

These Chaldeans would gather, together with their pupils, in the early evening. As the night grew dark, they sat in deep silence until, at the very hour of midnight, mysterious tones would sound for the and stream through the room, and a light would shine as if born out of the darkness. They called this "Seeing the Sun of the Midnight Hour." They had found the light in the moment of greatest darkness. Did it rise from within the darkness or from their inner selves?

To teach their pupils that this was the Light of Life, the priests would lead them into a cave where there seemed to be nothing but bare rock. There they saw stalks, bearing ears of grain, spring from the stones to proclaim the life that arises ever and forever from out of all that seems dead.

Over a thousand years later, there lived the three Magi, so called because they were great in wisdom. Old stories tell of their search among the clay tablets of the Chaldeans, where they found a prophecy that there would come a time, at the Midnight Hour, when two great stars would draw together in the constellation of the Fishes and that, in the darkness beneath them, a new star would appear, "the star of Jacob," to foretell that a new and greatest King would be born on earth: Christos, the very Being of the Sun! Thus, in the script of the Chaldeans, was announced the coming of the Light for the whole world which they had experienced in their celebration of the Night of Consecration.

It is told that the Magi spent three days every month, year after year, upon a high mountain, watching for the appearance of the star which had been foretold. Now, on the night of Christ's birth, a star appeared along with the form of a wondrous Child with a fiery cross upon his head, and it said to them: "Go in haste to Judea and there you will find a newborn child who is the King whom you await."

The rain has passed. With clouds gone by,
See the lights of the starry sky.

The forest is silent in dark of night.
Among wet leaves shines a tiny star-light.

As the glow-worm mirrors, what shines afar.

Orion's Belt? The Pleiades?
Stars as far away as these?

Between star of heaven and glow-worm spark,
The Christmas Star lights the dark of the heart.

Today's scientists now know that the Star of Bethlehem was probably a rising of Jupiter in early dawn (the East) between April 17 and December 19 in the year 6 BC. With Saturn nearby in a constellation associated with Judea, this would have signaled a regal birth that only serious astronomers of that time (i.e., the Magi) would have recognized. Later on, marking the years would be changed from BC (before Christus) to AD (*anno domini*, in the year of our Lord), to acknowledge this amazing moment in world history.

Some say it was the Child himself who led the Magi to the place of His birth. Some say it was a holy spirit who had taken this form in order to guide the Wise Men. Others think it was the angel, who also appeared to the shepherds. Yet others ask: Was it a heavenly body newly created that, once it had fulfilled its mission, was absorbed once more into the matter of the universe?

Saint Matthew wrote, "And lo, the star which they saw in the east went before them till it came and stood over where the young child was. And when they saw the star, they rejoiced with exceeding great joy."

Sennacherib and the Assyrians

To the north of Babylon stood the city of Assur. Built on a high bank of the Tigris River, it was easy to defend. The people of Assur were called the Assyrians. Their god was Assur, the god of war.

If we remember the Persians' description of Ahriman who led people toward war, we will understand the Assyrians. Unlike the Babylonians who were usually peaceful farmers and traders and whose priest-kings gave thought to building up an ordered world, the Assyrians were ones who tried to take over what others had built.

The first great Assyrian leader was a general who made himself king and took the name of Sargon, after the Semite king who had conquered the Sumerians. He led his armies far to the west, killing all who opposed him and then bringing home their cattle, grain, metals, jewelry and other treasures. He built a great city at Nineveh and a large palace for himself, more magnificent than any yet known, and then he filled the city and palace with stolen riches.

Sennacherib was his son and, when Sargon died, carried further the aims of his father to seize lands, cities and fields far beyond Assur and Nineveh. The name of Sennacherib came to be known and feared throughout the world. The Hebrew people, in the kingdom of Israel, were conquered by Sennacherib, their kingdom destroyed, and the people carried off to be slaves to the Assyrians.

The people in the Kingdom of Judah feared they too would be overcome; they feared that the god Assur might be stronger than the god of Israel and Judea. When the Assyrians reached the gates of Jerusalem, the people crowded the streets in fear. The prophet, Isaiah, stood before them and cried out that their god, Jehovah, was the Lord of all people and greater than Assur. Isaiah prophesied that the Assyrians, though they might win a few battles, would perish in the end. Strangely enough, sickness took hold of the soldiers in Sennacherib's armies, and they died by the hundreds. Jerusalem was saved.

Returning to Nineveh, Sennacherib built up a greater army and marched it down between the two rivers toward Babylon, burning cities on his way, killing thousands, capturing yet other thousands. His soldiers were archers, spearmen, and shield-bearers. They rode horses and drove chariots. They built great war machines on wheels, with battering rams that could knock down brick walls. The battering rams, spears and arrows were not all that was feared, for the soldiers themselves were cruel and fierce, devoid of human feelings. Wherever the terrible Assyrian armies swept through the land, they left a trail of ruin and death behind them.

Around smoking heaps, heaps that had once been towns and had been set on fire with Assyrian fire-brands, the leaders set up stakes on which they pinned the bodies of their victims who had been flayed alive. Yet others of those killed lay in mounds and piles all around to warn the world of what would happen to those who did not submit to the conquerors.

Nahum, another prophet of Judah, cried out against the Assyrians in these words, "Woe to the bloody city! It is all full of lies and robbery, the noise of the whip, the rattling of wheels, the prancing of horses and the jumping of chariots. The horsemen lifteth up both the bright sword and the glittering spear, and there is a multitude of the slain, and they stumble upon the dead. Behold I am against thee, saith the Lord of Hosts, and it shall come to pass that all they that shall look upon thee shall flee from thee and say, Nineveh is laid waste; who will bemoan her?"

So went Sennacherib and his armies until they came to Babylon, and utterly destroyed it. He let the waters from the canals, which had watered the barley fields, flood the ruins. Thus did the Assyrians come to be masters of the land between the rivers and far beyond—not through wisdom but by power. Instead of peaceful donkey caravans winding their way from town to town, and carrying grain and wool, the roads were choked with clouds of dust raised by great herds of cattle, horses, asses, goats and sheep, and long lines of camels laden with golden and silver treasure, all being driven toward Nineveh, whose king claimed the wealth of the people he had conquered.

Great was the wealth of Nineveh, now the center of the Assyrian Empire. The Assyrians were masters of the land between the rivers. They built great palaces and temples and laid out wondrous gardens with plants from all the conquered lands, even from India. Artists were brought to the city to decorate it with statues.

After Sennacherib died, his grandson, Assurbanipal, ruled the empire. He collected a great library of clay tablets (2200 of which were discovered centuries later in the ruins of Nineveh) on which were written the stories of the Assyrian triumphs.

Although for years this people ruled as conquerors, they had their troubles, for their subjects would revolt, and the leaders had to maintain large armies. They had to take farmers away from their fields, craftsmen away from their trades, merchants away from their businesses, and keep them in armies to subdue rebellions and to fight outsiders who came against Assyria from the north and from the south.

Soldiers do not grow food or build houses or weave robes. They do not produce anything for others but only use and eat up what others produce. Thus the time came in Assyria when fields went to waste, irrigation ditches broke down, trades were neglected and businesses suffered. Because of this, the Assyrians lost their strength. And when the Persians from the north and the Chaldeans from the desert lands to the south joined their armies and marched against Nineveh, they brought down the city walls, overthrew the hated Assyrians, and the prophecy of Nahum was fulfilled. All the surrounding nations rejoiced at the downfall of Nineveh, and it became the heap of rubbish it is today.

Then it came to pass that King Nebudchadnezzar, the Chaldean, rebuilt Babylon and Babylonia became part of Chaldea. It was Nebudchadnezzar who brought the people of Israel as captives to Babylon in 586 BC. His son, Belshazzar, was the last King of Babylon before it was captured by Cyrus the Great of Persia (538 BC), who allowed the captives from Israel to return to their own land.

The Chaldean kings spent many years digging in search of old documents. This was a looking backward. There was no new impulse. Their rule only lasted 68 years, from 606 BC to 538 BC.

Not all Assyrians were as ruthless as Sennacherib and his grandson. Here is an old story that has been told and retold about the son of Sennacherib, Esarhaddon:

Esarhaddon

KING OF ASSYRIA 681–668 BC
(from a story by Leo Tolstoy)

Esarhaddon, an Assyrian king, was the son of Sennacherib and the father of Assurbanipal. The Assyrians had conquered the realm of King Lailie, burned all the cities, slaughtered the warriors, and taken the inhabitants of this realm as slaves. Esarhaddon put King Lailie into a cage to keep him there until he could think of a good way to kill him.

At night, Esarhaddon lay in bed, thinking about putting King Lailie to death, when an old man appeared before him. "Do you wish to kill King Lailie?" asked the old man.

"Yes," answered Esarhaddon, "but I cannot decided by what means to execute him."

The old man said, "But you are Lailie."

"That is not true," replied Esarhaddon. "I am I, and Lailie is Lailie."

"You and Lailie are one," said the old man gently. "It only seems to you that you are not Lailie and that Lailie is not you."

"What do you mean 'seems'? Here I lie on a soft bed, surrounded by obedient slaves, and tomorrow I shall feast with my friends; whereas Lailie sits like a bird in a cage, and tomorrow he will be torn to pieces by my dogs."

"You cannot destroy his life," said the old man.

"If I can kill fourteen thousand of his warriors and build a hill with their bodies, I can destroy Lailie also."

"Come with me," said the old man, and he led Esarhaddon to a pool full of water. He filled a jug and said, "As soon as I begin to pour this water over you, put your head down all the way into the pool."

As he began to pour the jugful over Esarhaddon's head, the King did as he was told. No sooner was his head under water than he felt that he was no longer Esarhaddon but someone else. Before him was a beautiful woman he had never seen before, but he knew that she was his wife. She approached him, saying, "Lailie, my dear, the princes await you in the great hall. Go out to them."

Esarhaddon felt no surprise at her words and did as she bade him, going out to the great hall where princes awaited him to pay him their respects. They bowed before him and, at his command, arose and seated themselves to hold council. The eldest of the princes spoke, saying that they must wage war against the wicked Assyrian, King Esarhaddon; but "Lailie," as he now knew himself to be, did not agree. He commanded that ambassadors should go to King Esarhaddon, to plead with him. Then "Lailie" chose important princes to go on this mission and told them what to say.

Having dismissed the princes, Lailie-Esarhaddon rode forth to hunt, and after a successful one, he returned home to feast with his friends. The following day he held court. Many of the people of his realm came to him with requests and pleas for justice. After he had given judgments, he went hunting again, and again after the hunt, he feasted with his friends.

Thus he lived for days and weeks while waiting for the return of the ambassadors. At last they returned, but they had suffered a sad fate: Their noses and ears had been cut off. They brought the message to Lailie-Esarhaddon that what had been done to his ambassadors would be done to him too unless he, immediately, sent a tribute of silver, gold and cypress wood, and then came in person to pay homage to the Assyrian King.

Lailie, who was once Esarhaddon, called all princes together in council and they declared that they must now go to war against King Esarhaddon. Lailie agreed, took his place at the head of the army, and set out against the Assyrian. They marched for seven days, and each day Lailie rode among his men inspiring them with courage.

On the eighth day they met Esarhaddon's army in a broad valley on the banks of a river. As his warriors fought, Lailie saw Esarhaddon's armies swarming down from the surrounding hills. While Lailie's warriors could be numbered by the hundreds, Esarhaddon's were in the thousands. Lailie drove his war-chariot into the swarms of enemy soldiers, slashing and hewing at them with his sword.

Suddenly he felt that he had been wounded and he was taken prisoner. He marched for nine days with all the other captives and on the tenth day was brought to Nineveh and put into a cage where he sat for twenty days, suffering not only from his wound and from hunger but from shame and rage. He made up his mind not to let his enemies see his suffering and endured bravely all that happened, without a groan or a murmur, as his friends and relatives were led to be tortured, as his beloved wife also was led to Esarhaddon as a slave. He endured all this in silence.

Then came the day when two soldiers unlocked his cage and led him to a sharply-pointed stake. As they prepared to pierce his body through upon the stake, he forgot his resolve to remain calm and silent. He began to sob and pray for mercy, but no one listened to him. "This cannot be," he cried. "Surely it is a dream. I am not Lailie. I am Esarhaddon."

Then he heard a voice saying, "You are both Lailie and Esarhaddon."

As he felt that he was about to be pierced upon the stake, he cried out again and at the same instant raised his head from the pool of water. The old man was standing over him, emptying the last drops of water from the jug. "Oh, how terribly I have suffered! And how long!" said Esarhaddon.

"Long?" queried the old man. "You have only just dipped your head under water and raised it again. See, all the water has not even been poured from the jug. But do you now understand that Lailie is you, that you and Lailie are one? You thought life dwelt in you alone. Life is in everyone and everything as well as in you, and I have shown you that in doing evil to others, you have done it to yourself as well. With the portion of life that is in you, you can make all life better or worse." Having said this, the old man vanished.

The next morning King Esarhaddon commanded that Lailie and all the prisoners be freed. Then he summoned his son, Assurbanipal, and gave the kingdom over into his hands. He himself went into the wilderness to meditate on all that he had learned. Later he went through the towns and villages, preaching to people that all life is one and that men do evil to themselves in desiring to do evil to others.

[Note: In 1903, Tolstoy was asked for three stories for publication, the proceeds to help victims of an anti-Jewish pogrom. This story of Esarhaddon was one of the three.]

Egypt

Homage to thee, O Ra, when thou risest!
Thou stridest over the heavens in peace,
And all thy foes are cast down.
The never-resting stars sing hymns of praise to thee,
And the stars which rest and the stars which never fail
Glorify thee as thou sinkest to rest in the horizon of Manu,
O thou who art beautiful at morn and at eve.
   – Osiris the scribe Ani

Praise to thee, O Nile, that issuest forth from the earth
   and comest to nourish the dwellers in Egypt,
That waterest the meadows which Ra has created to nourish all cattle,
That giveth drink to the desert places which are far from water,
That maketh barley and createth wheat.
If he is sluggish, the nostrils are stopped up, and all men are brought low.
When he arises, earth rejoices, and all men are glad,
Every jaw laughs, and every tooth is uncovered.
Bringer of nourishment, creating all things good.
   – Hymn to the Nile

All cattle rest upon their pasturage.
The trees and plants flourish.
The birds flutter in their marshes,
Their wings uplifted in adoration to thee.
All the sheep dance upon their feet.
All winged things fly.
They live when thou has shone upon them.
The barques sail upstream and downstream alike.
Every highway is open because thou dawnest.
The fish in the river leap up before thee.
Thy rays are in the midst of the great green sea.
How manifold are thy works!
O sole god, whose powers no other possesseth.
   – selections from Akhnaton's *Hymn to the Sun*

To the Egyptian priests
the earth was not unreal,
nor was it evil,
but it was the work of the gods.
Everything in the world
was a footprint of the gods.
For them, the earth became
a very important place,
so important that they felt
all they did on earth
must be and could be
taken with them
to the spirit-world
when they died.
Since the earth showed forth
the being of the gods,
man could enjoy it.

The Wind and the Light

There was a time, when the world was in the midst of being created, when as yet there was no air and the men who lived upon the earth did not yet need to breathe. The earth was covered with misty vapors, within which the life-giving power of the sun was at work. The Sun-power and the mists were as one. The ancient Egyptians pictured two brothers, Osiris who was the Sun-power and his brother Set. The time came when Set separated himself from Osiris and, as the Wind, worked in the element of the air which now appeared, the moisture in the world-covering vapors shrank away. Osiris remained in the element of light.

Through the activity of Set, the air entered into man as breath; now mankind had to breathe. Before this moment men had lived without knowledge of birth and death. Now, as soon as he could breathe, man called breath "life," and the stopping of breath was "death."

The story of Osiris and Set was known by every Egyptian. It lived in his soul and reminded him that the moment of death, the stopping of breath, was to come to him and that he must learn during life how to enter into death.

Osiris

A long, long time ago, there lived a god-like king upon the earth, Osiris, the god of the Light. Everyone loved him and put his name above all names, for he was the life-giver, and he taught men how to be more than beggars and beasts by showing them how to use grain and grapes, by making laws, and by teaching men to look up to the gods. Under his rule all men lived in contentment.

Everyone loved him but for one who did not, and that was his brother Set. Set was the ruler of the desert where no plant grew. He it was who dried up the earth and made it uninhabitable. He was always up to his mischief, for his heart burned with a hot wind of hate for the green valleys of Osiris' kingdom and for anything that was alive.

Isis was the sister and wife of Osiris, and she was very watchful, always guarding Osiris from all harm. Osiris, however, set out to travel over the whole earth, to civilize it, to change mankind's way of life, not by use of arms and armies but by persuasion, reasoning, and songs of all kinds. He left Isis at home on guard against Set.

So long as Osiris was away, Set could not do anything against him because Isis was so watchful. But when Osiris returned, Set formed a plot against him to trick him.

Without Osiris' knowledge, Set measured Osiris' shadow, the height and the width, and had a beautiful chest made to fit the measure. Then he held a great banquet and invited everyone. All the guests admired the handsome and beautifully ornamented chest which had the shape of a man's form. Set announced, as if in sport, that he would give the chest as a present to the one who would lie down in it and exactly fit into it. Many tried. Some were too long, others too short, others too fat, others too thin. But when Osiris, full of merriment, lay in it, he fitted it exactly.

Set's seventy-two friends, who had plotted the trick with him, ran quickly to the chest, closed the lid and fastened it with nails, soldered it with melted lead, and carried it forth to the River Nile and let it float out to sea. As soon as Isis heard of it, she cut off a lock of her hair and put on a mourning robe. Then she set out to find Osiris.

She wandered over the earth for a long time. At last some children told her they had seen the chest floating toward the coast of a country named Byblos. Asking everyone she met, she made her way there. Finally she heard that a chest had been carried by the waves up onto the shore and it lay in the midst of a certain plant which had then grown so fast that it enfolded the chest within its trunk. The King of Byblos had noticed this unusually large tree and ordered it cut down for a pillar to support the roof of his palace.

Isis went to Byblos and became the nurse for the Queen's child. In time she revealed herself as a goddess and asked if she might have the pillar. When the King gave it to her, she took it away on a boat and returned to her own land. Once home, she hastened to greet her son, Horus, then but a baby, and left the chest unguarded. Set, out hunting by moonshine, came upon it and tore the body of Osiris into fourteen pieces which he hurled all over Egypt.

Hearing of this second evil, Isis again set out in a small boat and made her way through all of many swamps until she found all the parts of the body of Osiris and buried each at the place where she found it. She established a temple to Osiris at each burial place. Thus there came to be fourteen kingdoms in Egypt, instead of one.

Stricken with sorrow was Isis, and her cries awakened Osiris into the world of all who had died. Thereafter men on earth were comforted as they looked forward to death, when they would go to Osiris whose light shone for them in the realm of the dead. And so the living spoke of dying as "the coming forth into the light."

Now that Osiris had left the earth, who was to rule his kingdom? Set tried to win it for himself and would have done so but for Horus, the son of Isis and Osiris, who fought Set to avenge his father's death. It is said that the battle raged from one end of Egypt to the other, and, after eighty years of struggle, Horus finally overcame Set and assumed the throne.

Every Pharaoh of Egypt, after him, was known as the Living Horus. And when, at death, he moved to the "Land of the Western Ones," he took on the name Osiris.

The Biography of the River Nile

Westward from India across the Indian Ocean lies the great continent of Africa, and there, in the northern part, the sun blazes down day after day from a clear blue sky over yellow sands that stretch as far as the eye can see, to form the largest desert in the world. There is so little rain there that sometimes a whole year passes without a drop of water from the sky. A dry wind blows hot by day in the heat of the sun, but the nights are very cold. Few plants grow in the desert. It is mostly rock and sand, sand as bright and light as the sunshine, sand that is blown by the wind into hills that move and change like great ocean waves but, of course, more slowly.

Ever so long ago, at the time when the Babylonian priests were studying the stars and writing their clay tablet records, another people settled in this desert. They settled in a place where there was plenty of water because of the river that flowed through the sandy, dry desert, a river that never dried up. They, too, built their houses of sun-dried brick and cultivated the earth in the river valley. One could ask, "Even with all the water in the world, how could anything grow in sand?"

Where did the river come from in a land where there was no rain? Why didn't it dry up? How could people make bricks for their houses out of anything but clay? How could they plant wheat and barley and make it grow without good, rich earth?

In these early days, the Egyptians did not know where the river came from. It flowed northward from the south. In their boats, the people could sail to the south just to a certain place—and no further. There the river was crowded with great rocks and stones that lay about like huge hippopotamuses, their wet backs rising from the swirling water to glisten in the sun.

If people traveled beyond this, without boats, they came to other rocky rapids or cataracts, six altogether, and beyond them the river would still be flowing from further south, so far that in those days none could explore it. The people said that the river was part of the Heavenly Stream which surrounds the earth and which never could dry up.

Yet more wonderful, the river brought not only water to this land but it brought rich, black earth. Every year, at the same season, high waves of water would dash down past the cataracts in such a flood that the river would rise up over its banks and the water would spread out on either side to cover the land for miles. The flood waters were dark with a fine, black, muddy silt. After about two months, the floods would sink down again and leave behind a new, fresh layer of black earth on the ground. Thus, these early people found, along the shores of the river, many layers of deep, black soil. When seeds were cast into the mud right after the floods receded, they would grow so fast that the people could harvest their crops just two months after they had been planted.

The people said that these two gifts of water and soil were sent down to them by the Nile-God who, somewhere far off to the south, knelt in a rocky cavern underground. They pictured him with a sacred vessel in each hand, pouring forth the life-giving floods of water and new earth. Thus they could cultivate and draw their food from the earth, and from the mud they could shape bricks and harden them in the hot sun and build houses.

There remains another question: How did the Egyptians manage to water their crops in the ten months between floods when the hot, dry winds from the desert took all the moisture even from along the shores of the river?

What the gods gave them, they cherished and gave thanks, but they didn't let the gods do everything. They did something for themselves. After the floods subsided, the people lifted the water from the river up on to the land and let it flow through trenches into ponds and tanks where they stored it between banks of earth, to be used as they needed it. And how did they lift the water? With water wheels, well sweeps and dams.

Today we can follow the River Nile and find its sources. About two hundred years ago someone did so, but this is very recent when we think that for five thousand years the people of the Nile did not know what we can easily know now.

Today, from the mouth of the River, we would have to travel four thousand miles to the south to reach the southernmost source. If we traveled at the same rate that it takes the water from this source to reach the Mediterranean Sea, it would take us four months (at the rate of one thousand miles a month). The distance and time have been measured by means of high water marks as the Nile moves north during the flood season. This river is the second longest in the world—and one of the most interesting.

Imagine two brothers who, unlike Osiris and Set, start out separately and become one. One of them is quiet, calm and slow moving, patient and determined to get to the end of his journey in his own good time. The other is wilder: He hurls himself along, dragging everything with him as he leaps down cliffs, rushes between crowded rocks, roars and shouts on his way as if he feared to be late. These two brothers are the two sources of the Nile: The slow, quiet one rises and starts out from a great, calm lake in the highlands far to the south. The wild one comes down from among the peaks of old volcanoes, to the northeast of the first. As the calm one winds its way through thick forests, it gathers plant substances in its stream; old logs, leaves, roots and fruits float down upon it and dissolve in it. As the wild one tears down the crumbly sides of volcanic mountains, it washes away the minerals and metals that have boiled up out of the earth in distant ages and carries them along with it, grinding and stirring them into the fine mud we call silt.

The calm one flows night and day from out of the great lake, or inland sea. Daily rainstorms keep the lake full. The wild one darts down from his volcanoes only at a certain time each year and in such torrents that people and animals have to flee away to save their lives, should they be wandering near this source. The time for the river to leap down the mountains comes when winds from the southeast storm up the mountain sides. They are full of moisture from the Atlantic Ocean where they begin. They gather more moisture as they dance over the hot, wet jungles of South Africa for a thousand miles. When they reach the mountains and dash up their high slopes to the cold air among their peaks, the load of sea moisture and land moisture fall in torrents of rain. The wild river catches the rain and comes to life! This happens every year in April, and four months later this wild being reaches the Mediterranean Sea. Then in June the dry northeast winds blow down from over the deserts and put the wild brother to sleep until the next spring.

To the north of their sources, the two brothers meet and become one, flowing as one for 1350 miles more to carry their treasures to Egypt, treasures of plant and mineral substances which they will leave on the land as fine, new earth. The calm brother, with the clearest water, is called the White Nile. The wild brother, with almost black water, is the Blue Nile. After they become one, they are the River Nile flowing north to the Land of Egypt.

Just as farmers in other lands look up to the sky for signs of rain, so the Egyptians look into the distance toward the south, each year in July, for the flood wave riding down the bed of their one river. The White Nile would never overflow its banks without the Blue, but without the White, the Blue Nile would let the plants of Egypt die of thirst in the months between the floods.

Khufu

PHARAOH OF EGYPT around 3000 BC

Khufu was a young noble of Egypt who owned much land. He spent his days hunting and swimming and overseeing the work on his estates. He had become learned in temple wisdom for, as a boy, he had gone through the temple school.

Not everyone went to school in Egypt. Those who did had to show, not how much they knew nor how clever they were, but whether or not they had courage, whether or not they could finish what they started, and whether or not they could bear to feel all alone. Their courage, devotion and self-reliance were tested before their studies could begin.

The schools were in the temples, and the teachers were the priests who were the real leaders of Egypt, for they even guided and advised the kings and Pharaohs. The common people—farmers, traders and craft-workers—were in turn guided by those who had been educated in the temple schools. The temples were also the dwelling places of Ra, the Sun God. The image of Ra was placed in a special room where none but the priests could enter. Once a year it was taken out of the room and carried in a boat on the River Nile, to bless it.

When Khufu went to enter the temple school for the first time, he did not know that one day he would be the ruler of the lands around the River Nile. At the temple entrance he was met by a priest who looked into the boy's eyes, as if searching into every corner of his heart and soul to find out if there was any fear or untruth, any selfishness or meanness hiding there, Khufu looked straight back into the eyes of the priest without ever looking away, down or up, or to one side or another. Then the priest led the boy further into the temple.

Once inside, Khufu faced a gateway between two pillars. One pillar was red and the other black. The red pillar marked "the way of light," the black one "the way of darkness." Standing with Khufu before the pillars, the priest said, "You now have to make up your mind to step forward through this portal, for once you have passed these pillars there is no turning back. You will then have to stay in the temple for three-times-seven years. That is the length of the time for the temple training. If, after passing the portal you choose not to continue your training, yet you will have to remain here as a slave for the same length of time."

Khufu did not hesitate to pass between the pillars. He was led into a room where he saw a veiled statue under which was written: "No one has ever lifted my veil." Standing before this mysterious figure he had to vow that for the next seven days he would not speak a word. Then he was led into another room. The door to this room closed heavily behind him, and he knew for certain there was no turning back. He found out that he was now all alone and facing a passageway through which he could, and must, go—for it was the only way ahead.

As he stepped along this passageway, it became darker and narrower until he could barely squeeze through. At length he came into a larger room again. Here he found no other way to go ahead except down some steps into a well.

Now he had to enter the water. As he was sinking into it, he discovered a small hole through which he crawled into another room where he could see no way ahead but only the hole leading back into the well.

Knowing that there was no turning back, he remained in the room. Now he felt an overpowering sense of loneliness, the kind of loneliness that people must feel when they are dying with no one to help them. He wanted to cry out for help but remembered his vow of silence and kept still. That was the right choice for, in due course, a door opened in what had seemed to be a solid wall, and he could leave the room of loneliness. Through the open door, however, he saw a room full of flames. With no other choice but to enter it, when he did, he found that the flames were not real but mirrored.

These tests of his physical courage were easy ones compared with others that followed. But he passed them and was admitted to the studies in the temple school and was taught by the priests in many fields of knowledge of the world: knowledge of minerals, plants, medicine, architecture, music, astronomy.

His teachers divided his time between the instruction they gave and his meditation on what they had taught. He was asked to think and live in what they taught until he really understood. Often he felt deserted and discouraged. True wisdom seemed out of reach, and he would ask silently, "When will I be allowed to see the light of Osiris?" only to get the answer, "Work and pray!" Sometimes he would be given help and encouragement, and he enjoyed his progress, until the day came when he was told that he was ready to go through the initiation that would make him a priest of Osiris.

In the evening the priests, bearing torches, accompanied him to a crypt deep within the temple. There they instructed him to lie down in a marble sarcophagus. They comforted him, telling him not to be afraid, for they said, "You are already one of our brothers." The high priest blessed him, and then the procession of priests silently left him.

Khufu heard voices singing a funeral chant in the distance. Gradually he fell into a deathlike sleep during which pictures of his lives on earth passed before him as in a dream. A beautiful white rose bloomed and unfolded and took the form of Isis. Then a glorious light shone around and within him, for he had entered the kingdom of Osiris and was filled with the wisdom for which he had worked and studied for three-times-seven years.

After three days, Khufu awakened and was able to remember and speak about what he had experienced in the realm of Osiris. Thus he became a priest of Osiris, able to teach and guide the people in the land of Egypt. And, in due time, he was selected by the other priests as Pharaoh.

As soon as he became Pharaoh, Khufu started to build his tomb, high on the desert hills above the Royal City to the west of the Nile, a site now known as the old town of Giza. A hundred thousand men worked for him to quarry and move the stones for the *mastaba* (or "house of eternity") which was to be his tomb, along with his commissioning of the Great Pyramid. First he had to find rocks, the right kind, but they were so far away that it took ten years just to build the road along which to move the rocks. Every three months a new army of a hundred thousand men would replace the old. How did they move the rocks? How did they lift them with no machines such as we have today? An overseer, with a whip, cracked out a rhythm; the blocks were pulled and pushed on rollers, up ramps, with a great strength that came to the workers through the rhythmic pulling and pushing together. The workmen lived in temporary cities where the work went on and were paid only in corn and wine. The rocks were lifted up to desert heights and then up to the pyramid heights. This took another twenty years.

No such building as the Great Pyramid was ever reared before or after, although later pharaohs erected their smaller pyramids stretching for sixty miles in a long line to the south. None was so great as Khufu's. It was 480 feet high, approximately 755 feet square at the base, and consisted of an estimated 2.3 million blocks of limestone and granite. It covered 13 acres, or three city blocks. From its blocks of stone, each weighing 15–20 tons, a big city could have been built. These great blocks were fitted together so neatly, without cement, that one could not push the edge of a piece of paper through the cracks.

Inside this great, manmade mountain of stone, long passages lead to two small rooms in the center of the pyramid. There, many scientists now think, is where the very best students, in turn, would lie in the stone sarcophagus, in the midst of the darkness, until awakened as initiates. The chamber was named *Khut*, meaning "Glory. Light in Darkness"!

What other wonders are known about this pyramid? It was built on uneven ground, so an exact measure of the base from corner to corner is impossible. Yet the four corners are exactly square and the four sides exactly the same length. Four shining and exact triangles rose to a center exactly above the center of the base. The center stones were covered with polished limestone and tipped with gold to catch the rays of the sun. Each face of the pyramid was exactly in line with the north, south, east and west. The passageways to the central chamber came from the surface on the east and west to catch the rays of the rising and setting sun so that the *Ka*, or spirit of the student, could enter the chamber at sunrise and depart to Osiris at sunset.

The People of Egypt

Every ruler of Egypt was known as the "Living Horus" and was often represented as a falcon. The Egyptian word *Hor* means "sky," and the people thought of the sky as a divine falcon whose two eyes were the sun and the moon. The Egyptians thought of their Pharaoh as the son of the Sun. Whenever a Pharaoh appeared among his people, a great cry went before him: "Earth, beware, your god comes!" Every person, of high or low degree, had to bow to the earth when he approached the Pharaoh on any matter, and kiss the ground where his feet had rested. The most highly favored were allowed to kiss the Pharaoh's foot.

This god-like being had much to do with the land, and the people wanted to be sure that, as he grew older, he had no weakness in him. After thirty years of reigning, he was required to prove that he still had the strength to rule his people. He had to appear before all the nobles who represented the gods attending the supreme God, Pharaoh. Then one who represented Thoth gave the Pharaoh a cup containing "the elixir of youth." Having drunk the liquid, the Pharaoh would run a race to prove his strength.

How did he rule? He owned the land of Egypt, and all who lived and worked there had to give him a part of what they harvested or made. Under him were those who helped him rule his kingdom. There were the priests who made maps of the heavens, naming the stars. Working with certain instruments they marked out the fields according to the positions of the stars in the sky, so that the boundaries could not be forgotten after the flood had drowned the land. There were the scribes who wrote accounts and kept records. There were overseers who saw to it that the laborers did their daily work in the building of tombs and temples. And over them all, closest to the Pharaoh, was the one who saw to it that the kingdom and the affairs of the king really prospered, the Vizier.

In 2900 BC, Egypt was a rich and busy land with the people engaged in many trades. Coppersmiths made vessels and tools, especially big saws for cutting stone blocks. Goldsmiths fashioned golden jewelry. Stone workers made stone bowls that were ground so thin that light shone through them. Potters made wine jars. Weavers made fine, transparent linen like silk. Paper makers made the first paper in history out of papyrus reeds. Ship builders made the boats for the River Nile. Carpenters made furniture and mummy cases. Traders sailed the river and carried these wares, even out to sea to other lands. And of course there were the farmers, who worked the fields, dug the canals and irrigation ditches, and kept them full.

Every year, the Pharaoh would write something on a scroll of papyrus, reminding the River Nile of its duties toward the land and asking that the River be put into a kindly mood. He would throw the scroll, together with sacrifices, into the waters. And every year, after the flood had brought its gifts to the land, the Pharaoh would command that the *Apis* (sacred bull) be brought out and driven around the walls of city to make the fields fertile. Then the sowing of seed began. The people, wearing strings of onions around their necks, sang as they worked.

Every day the Pharaoh's Vizier would rise to go forth to see how well the Pharaoh's subjects were carrying out the Pharaoh's affairs. His servants hastened to dress him. One carefully placed a wig on his head so that his face would have a dignified frame. Another put embroidered sandals on his feet. Four dwarfs arranged his collar, which was a sign of his high rank. Others brought him scrolls on which were written the business he must conduct. And as he was being readied for the day, nearby musicians played on harps and flutes to put him in a good mood. He assigned the day's work to those who were responsible for one thing or another and then, after breakfasting on fragrant fruit, set out to inspect the work of the men who were engaged in keeping the canals and ditches in order, or cutting grain, or tending cattle.

The Vizier was carried in a litter, for a man of his high office was not allowed to touch his embroidered sandals to the bare ground. As they toiled along, his bearers chanted, "We would rather have the litter full than empty."

It is a bustling life that meets the Vizier as he is carried about in his litter: Two field workers are caught secretly milking a cow. One says, "Hurry, the herdsman is coming!" But it is too late. The herdsman rains blows on their shoulders. Some sailors by a canal are fighting and one of them shouts, "Break his head open. There's not much in it anyhow!" Some shepherds are driving their herds from one pasture to another through the mud left by flood waters and testing the slippery ground with their crooks. One says, "How fitting for shepherds to visit the fish and ask after their health!"

Chanting magic spells to frighten crocodiles that may be lurking in the water, some cowherds are trying to drive their cattle across flooded land. The cows don't think much of this and refuse to move. Then one man takes a calf on his back and wades in. The mother of the calf splashes after her baby, and the other cows follow her.

Fish are being dried, grapes harvested, grain cut and threshed under the hooves of donkeys. Rams are being driven over freshly-sown fields so that their sharp hooves will drive the seed into the soft earth. Carpenters are sawing logs. Stone masons are hewing blocks of stone. Potters are shaping jars on their wheels. Some serving maids are using hand mills to grind grain; one calls, "A little faster if you can!" Another answers, "I am working as fast as I can."

In the market place there is a lot of noise. Merchants are calling their wares: "Hot cakes, still hot!" "Linen, sandals, first class goods!" "Oil, oil! How much is a jug of oil?"

The Vizier enjoys all the bustle and the noise and thinks, *It is all a sign of good government.* Yes, thinks the Vizier, *everywhere there is an outpouring of life like the waters of the Nile.*

Last of all he sees a man in a boat hunting hippos with a harpoon. The man's wife sits in the boat and holds her husband firmly by one leg so that he won't fall overboard when he hurls the weapon.

When the Vizier returns to make his report to the Pharaoh, the King reminds him, "The Vizier is the copper wall that surrounds the King's golden house. Your eye and your ear must be the same to all who stand high and to those whose tables are empty and who only own one apron. You stand in a public place. Wind and water speak of you. What you do cannot remain hidden.

Remember that a man lives on after his death. His deeds will be heaped up like mountains beside him!"

Where did this story of the Vizier come from? From pictures and writings on the walls of his tomb. So greatly did the Egyptians love life that even before they died, they built their own tombs and employed artists to paint the stories of their lives on the walls of their tombs.

Life and Death

In the universe of earth and sun, moon and stars, the people of Egypt felt the presence of Divine Beings. The rich floods of the Nile, the desert, the crocodile, the cow, the lotus flower, the hawk—the whole physical world in fact was a story written by the gods. Happy was the soul who could be helped to remember his wondrous life on earth after he had died. Yet, only if he had lived rightly could he enter the shining realms of Osiris after death.

Guided by Anubis, a jackal-headed god, to the Hall of Truth, he would come before forty-two judges, each one having the power to judge one of forty-two sins. If the soul could say that he was guilty of none, he would be led by Horus to the throne where Osiris awaited him to welcome him to the fields of contentment. As the soul answered each of the forty-two questions, the god Thoth weighed his heart against the feather of truth from the headdress of Maat, the goddess of truth. If the scale showed that the heart was no heavier than the feather, then it was judged that he spoke truly. But a heavier heart was one burdened by misdeeds in life.

The Egyptians provided the body of one who had died with a tomb which was built to last forever. The walls of a wealthy burial chamber were covered with writings and paintings depicting the dead person's life on earth. His earthly possessions were arranged in surrounding rooms. His body was embalmed so that it would not turn to dust. Thus the *Ka* (spirit) of the dead person could always look into earthly life and find reminders there as to who he had been and what he had done. So it was that the biography of every noble person was shown in his burial place.

Ancient and Early Greece

A PRAYER:
Beloved Pan,
And all ye other gods who haunt this place,
Give beauty in the inward soul,
And may the outer and the inward man
Be at one.
> – Socrates

Here on earth, between birth and death,
The soul and spirit must be sought for in the body.
> – Rudolf Steiner, *Principles of Greek Education*

What is beautiful must also be right and true.
> – Aristotle, *Ethics*

The Greek gods had human passions, human faults,
Human sympathies and antipathies.
The Greeks were aware that their gods
Had the same advantage to derive
From earthly evolution as man himself.
> – Iamblichus

The heroes were to teach man
How to become an individual
Through the gifts of freedom.
> – Ralph Waldo Emerson

The Greeks were masters at capturing
The harmony and beauty of the human form,
In motion and at rest, and at conveying
The strength and dignity of the individual.
> – *Hegel's* Aesthetics

The story of the human being now leads us
to a time when they inhabited the earth
with so much more interest that
the world after death became for them
a "land of the shades," dim and unreal.
Even the gods dwelt within the world of humans
and took part in their affairs.
The gods lived on the mountaintops,
in the rivers, in the forests, in the seas,
and often married mortals that
great heroes might be born to lead the people.

Orpheus

Orpheus with his lute made trees
And the mountaintops that freeze,
Bow themselves when he did sing:
To his music plants and flowers
Ever sprung; as sun and showers
There had made a lasting spring.
— William Shakespeare. *Henry V*

When India was entering the Kali Yuga, and its ancient glories were dying away, Assyria had conquered Babylonia and was treading Asia underfoot. This was the age of Moses. The Egyptian priests and Pharaohs were strong but did not have much influence beyond Egypt. In Greece there had lived, for thousands of years, a white race, now mingled with many other peoples from India, Egypt and Phoenicia. The language of Greece was a mixture of Zend, Sanskrit, and Celtic. It imitated all the voices of nature, from the chirping of birds to the roar of the storm wind and the murmur of waves against the shores of the land.

To the north and east of the Aegean Sea was Thrace, a wild and rugged land. Chains of mountains were covered with giant oaks and topped with rocks. High among these mountains were temples to the gods: Kronos, Zeus, and Uranos. There the Sun was worshiped and Apollo, the god of light. The priests were men. Deep in the valleys and forests between the mountain peaks lived worshipers of Hecate, the goddess of magic, who, together with other powers, could send demons to the earth to torment men. Her temple was served by women, priestesses who were called Bacchantes, and they were the enemies of Zeus and Apollo. Woe to the priest who came to spy on the Bacchantes! He would be torn to pieces.

At this time, a young man of royal race appeared in Thrace. He was said to be the son of Apollo. His musical voice charmed all who heard it. His golden hair fell about his shoulders, and his deep blue eyes shone with such power, sweetness and magic that the fierce Thracians fled from his glance. Even the Bacchantes were subdued by his beauty and slunk around him and smiled at his words without being able to understand them.

Orpheus was the great hero of Thrace, not a hero for his warlike deeds but for his musical gifts. He played the lyre and sang so marvelously that wild beasts came running to listen "and even the trees would follow him." The dark spirits of the world were soothed and calmed by his sweet voice.

Orpheus loved and married a sweet nymph, a maiden named Eurydice, and they dwelt together in great happiness until, one day, Eurydice was bitten by a snake hidden in the grass and died. Her soul went to the Land of the Shades, where go all those who die. Heartbroken, Orpheus resolved to go there to find her.

With his music he was able to charm Hades, the king of the underworld, and was given permission to take Eurydice back to earth on the condition that he not turn back to look at her during the journey. Orpheus agreed and, followed by his beloved Eurydice, set out to return to the earth through a long, dark tunnel. They had nearly reached their destination and Orpheus could see daylight at the end of the tunnel, when he became anxious to see if Eurydice was following, and he turned his head, only to see her vanish as she was whisked back to Hades.

When the grief-stricken Orpheus disappeared from Thrace suddenly, he was said to have died. However he had secretly fled to Egypt and entered a Temple School in Memphis. After 21 years he returned, having been through the Egyptian teachings, and he bore a name given him by his Egyptian teachers: Orpheus of Arpha, which means "one who heals with light."

> *Eurydice alive would have given me supreme happiness;*
> *Eurydice dead made me find truth.*
> *It was with love that I put on the robe of linen,*
> *that I sought divine knowledge;*
> *that I climbed the walls of the pyramids*
> *and entered the tombs of Egypt.*
> *I searched death to find life;*
> *The priests of Isis and Osiris gave their secrets to me.*
> *They had only those gods; I had Eros!*
> *Through him I spoke, sang and conquered!*
> *Through him I pronounced the word of Zeus and Apollo!*
>   – excerpts from "The Death of Orpheus"
>   chapter 29, *The Great Initiates* by Édouard Schuré

When Orpheus returned to Thrace, the old priests of a mountain temple welcomed him as their leader, and he became the high priest of Zeus and Apollo. Later the worship of Orpheus spread throughout Greece.

One day, as the priests were performing their sacrificial ritual in the temple, Orpheus led a Greek child from the temple to teach him about the mysteries of the gods. Orpheus wore a robe of white linen, a golden belt flashing with dark crystals and a crown of myrtle leaves; he carried in one hand an ebony scepter with an ivory head. The boy, who was a pupil in the temple, was pale and trembling as he awaited the teaching of his master. Orpheus saw this and, to reassure him, put his arm gently around the boy's shoulders. While the priests could be heard singing a hymn of the fire, Orpheus spoke to his pupil:

"Hear the first mystery. A single Being rules in the deep sky and in the abyss of earth, the thundering Zeus, the ethereal Zeus. He rules in the depths of the earth and the heights of the starry sky. He is the very breath of things. Zeus is the creative fire, and when the lightning falls, it bursts from his right hand.

"Hear, now, the second mystery. Zeus is the great Demiurge. Dionysos is his son, his Word made manifest. Dionysos was the splendor of his father's habitation, the eternal palace of ether.

"One day, Dionysos looked into the depths of the heavens through the stars and saw, reflected in the blue abyss, his own image extending its arms toward him. Fascinated, he tried to grasp it, but the image fled from him. He followed it until, at length, he found himself in a shadowy, fragrant valley where, in a grotto, he saw the goddess Persephone weaving a marvelous tapestry upon which he could see pictures of all beings moving to and fro. As he gazed, enraptured, at the beauteous goddess, the Titans saw him.

"Jealous of his beauty were the Titan gods. Madly in love with him were the Titan goddesses. So the Titans threw themselves upon him, tore him to pieces, and distributed the parts of his body among themselves. They burned these and they buried his heart.

"But Zeus hurled his thunderbolts and struck the Titans, while his daughter, Pallas Athena, carried the heart of Dionysos into the clouds where it became a glowing sun.

"This is the mystery of the death of Dionysos. Now hear the mystery of his resurrection. Humans are the flesh and blood of Dionysos: Unhappy people are the scattered parts of his body, which seek for each other, in pain and love, through thousands of lives. From the smoke of Dionysos' body came the souls of human beings, and when they ascend into heaven, they will rejoin the flaming heart of Dionysos like torches, and Dionysos will be more alive than ever in the heights of heaven."

Thus spoke Orpheus to his pupil: "May Zeus and Dionysos be kind to your youth and pour into your heart the knowledge of the gods, for the hour of my death draws near. Once more must I descend into Hell to ascend into Heaven."

As Orpheus and his pupil approached the edge of the forest, they came upon a troop of Thracian Bacchante warriors encamped there. The leaders surrounded Orpheus, crying, "Who are you? What have you come here for?"

Orpheus responded by singing, "Kings, leaders, warriors of Thrace, the gods from above speak to you through me. Good are their deeds! Serve ye divine Apollo and Ethereal Zeus. Then shall the strife on earth be lessened, then shall the sick be healed, then shall the seeds of knowledge bring forth divine fruits of life: joy, love and beauty."

As Orpheus sang, the Bacchantes crept out from the shadows of the forest and drew near to sit at his feet like tamed beasts, all except Aglaonice, their high priestess, who lurked at the forest's edge and refused to listen to his singing. A warrior announced, "A god is speaking! Apollo himself is charming the Bacchantes."

Aglaonice darted forward, screaming, "A god, you say? Well, I say he is Orpheus, a man like yourselves who is deceiving you. A god you say? The son of Apollo? Throw yourselves upon him. If he is a god, let him defend himself."

Other warriors cried, "Let him defend himself if he be a god!" They drew their swords and struck him down. Now did that valley moan and mountains and deep forests groan like a great lyre. Priests bore his body then far from the world of men to a funeral pyre. And his immortal soul rose to its predestined goal through flames of fire to heaven. This ends the story of Orpheus, who gave joy to the earth through singing.

The Greek Gods and the Beginning of All Things

EREBUS, a being of darkness, and NYX, a being of night, together made a great egg from which EROS, love, came forth to create GAEA, the earth. Then Gaea created URANUS, heaven, to surround and protect her.

Uranus and Gaea became the first rulers of heaven and earth. They had twelve gigantic children, the TITANS, six sons and six daughters. Uranus feared they would use their great strength against him, so he cast them down into a dark abyss under the earth, from whence they made a hideous clamor for freedom. Gaea begged Uranus to free them. When he refused, she descended into the abyss and persuaded Kronos, the youngest Titan, to overthrow Uranus. This he did with the help of the scythe which Gaea made for him. After his defeat, Uranus cursed Kronos and prophesied that the day would come when Kronos would be overcome by his own children.

KRONOS, the father of time, took over the throne of Uranus and chose RHEA, a sister Titan, for his wife. He made the other Titans rulers over the different parts of the world. Fearful of his father's prophecy, Kronos swallowed all his children except the youngest, ZEUS, whom Rhea hid from Kronos; she gave him a stone instead. Zeus grew up and defeated his father. Rhea brewed a drink for Kronos which made him vomit up the children he had swallowed.

Zeus banished all the Titans who would not submit to his rule and then divided up the kingdoms of the earth among his brothers and sisters. He chose HERA, a sister of his, to be his Queen. Among the brothers and sisters of Zeus were: POSEIDON, god of seas and rivers; HADES, god of the underworld, the kingdom of the dead; DEMETER, goddess of agriculture and all the fruits of the earth; and HESTIA, goddess of the hearth and home.

Zeus became the Ruler of Heaven and Earth. Although Hera was Queen of Heaven, she was not Zeus' only wife, for Zeus "married" many other goddesses and even mortal maidens, which made Hera very angry. Hera avenged her wrongs in many ways, for she was jealous of all who were favored by the great Zeus. Zeus had seven children, four sons and three daughters:

APOLLO, god of the sun, of instrumental music, poetry and all the arts; HERMES, the messenger of the gods; ARES, the god of war, who took charge of all battles; HEPHAESTUS, the god of the forge, skilled in the art of working all metals in his workshop among the ever-burning fires in the depths of the earth; ATHENA, goddess of wisdom, of the peaceful arts and of defensive war; APHRODITE, goddess of love, who watched over all love and marriages; and ARTEMIS, goddess of the moon, who rode the heavens by night and, as goddess of the hunt, hunted on earth by day. Other sons of Zeus, born of mortal women, were the demi-gods (or half-gods) Heracles, Dionysos, and Perseus.

High on Mount Olympus lived the gods. They visited the earth often to bring help and protection to mankind, and sometimes dissent and destruction as well.

King Minos of Crete

While the great pyramids of Egypt were being built, Egyptian merchants were sailing their ships to the island of Crete, which lies across the entrance to the Aegean Sea. Crete was said to be the birthplace of Zeus, the ruler of the gods, who by a mortal woman had a son, Minos, who became the King of Crete. The name Minos fitted him, for he had a "mind" of his own. His palace was in the city of Knossos, or "knowledge."

When Poseidon, the god of the sea, sent Minos a special white bull to slay as a sacrifice to all the gods, Minos kept it for himself, as if he had the thought, *Why should I give the bull's powers to the gods? I will keep them.*

Poseidon found out that Minos had disregarded the gods and, to punish him, sent him the Minotaur, a monster with the head of a bull, a monster of darkness that fed on human beings. With the help of clever Daedalus who designed a labyrinth of mysterious passages, King Minos imprisoned the Minotaur therein, and fed the monster, not the people of Crete but those from the conquered city of Athens.

King Minos was interested in the inventions of the human mind, and he employed Daedalus of Athens who, as well as creating the labyrinth, designed and built reservoirs, theaters, tools for ship-building, and the masts for sails on ships. Defying Poseidon, Minos built a fleet of ships, by means of which he conquered Athens and all the islands of the Aegean Sea.

Crete lies between Egypt and Greece both as to its location and its place in history. It was a meeting place of an old and a new time. The navy of Minos carried on trade with Egypt as well as Greece.

From Egypt, the Cretans obtained copper and tin and combined them to get a metal harder than copper—bronze, from which they made weapons and the bronze ax used in ship building. From Egypt they also learned how to fashion clay jars and vases and decorated them so beautifully with plant forms that the Egyptians sought to buy them to place in the tombs of their kings. The Cretans also learned glassmaking from the Egyptians.

To Greece, the Cretan ships carried works of Cretan and Egyptian art, pottery, tiles, woolens, jewels, bronze weapons, and armor. The Greek city of Mycenae, a hilltop fortress built around the palaces of its princes, was filled with treasures from Crete and Egypt: golden doors and golden statues; furniture inlaid with gold, silver and ivory; gold and silver drinking cups and basins; and fine weavings.

Knossos, the city of King Minos, was excavated by Sir Arthur Evans in the late 19th century. Wall paintings in the palace of Minos picture the life of the Cretans before Minos was king. The throne of the king was found and the palace unearthed and partially restored. It appeared as a maze of rooms with only three entrances. Many writings on clay tablets were found. Some in a language called Linear B have been translated; these tablets are a record of Crete's trade. Other tablets have writing called Linear A; no one as yet has been able to decipher this writing. On one round tablet, called the Phaiston disc, the writing or little pictures are arranged in spirals on both sides; this writing too is still a great mystery to archaeologists!

From archaeological discoveries, we now know that early Crete was probably a matriarchy. The wall paintings show men bringing gifts to a woman called the Snake Goddess. Also the art of Crete is full of curves and flowers, which some think indicate a strong feminine influence. Both men and women practiced the sport of leaping over running bulls. The Palace of Knossos also has many symbolic bull-horn ax images all over, indications that Minos probably conquered Crete.

The "hidden story" in what we know of King Minos can be told in this way: Minos was headstrong. He thought for himself. He was eagle-like but wanted to have the power of the bull also. He marked a time when human beings were beginning to feel god-like powers within themselves, and Minos tried to wield more power than the gods. Yet he did not keep his power. Was it because he was defiant?

A new people, the Dorian Greeks, took the place prominence from the Egyptians and Cretans in the Mediterranean World. Their gods were important to them; they were often the fathers or mothers of humans, who lent the people a part of their god-nature so that they could become god-like, or more heroic. Many were the heroes of Greece: part god, part mortal. The gods favored their mortal children, lent them power in battle, fought behind them and against each other through the humans. The affairs of the gods were very much connected with the affairs of the people on earth, for the earth had become an important place.

Theseus

The Aegean Sea is like a large lake, and the island of Crete lies to the south like a guardian at the entrance of the Sea, halfway between Egypt and Greece. The Aegean Sea is so thick with islands that one sails across the Sea with some island always in view. It takes only an hour or two to sail from one island to another. Here, around the Sea, the world is beautiful. The islands rise out of the blue water like jewels sparkling in the sunshine. The coastlines are deeply indented with many bays and harbors. The mountains and headlands lift high their cloud-capped peaks into the blue sky.

How did the Aegean Sea get its name? In the Heroic Age of Greece, there was once a king named Aegeus. When he was young, he traveled to a far land and married a pretty, young princess named Aethra, and to them a son was born. They named him Theseus. While Theseus was yet a baby, King Aegeus had to return to his kingdom. Under a great rock, he hid his shining sword and golden sandals, and told Aethra that when their son was grown-up and strong enough to lift the rock, he should take the sword and sandals from under it and bring them to his father in Athens.

After a time, Theseus became a great, strong youth with golden hair and a hero's bearing. His mother took him to the secret rock, and he was able to lift it up. There he discovered his father's sword and golden sandals, still shining with the same glory as on the day they were hidden there. Then Aethra told Theseus to go to his father, the King of Athens, and make himself known by means of these precious tokens.

Theseus set forth. He decided to go the most dangerous way, by land and on foot. He met many monstrous and cruel giants and had to fight them. In each battle, Theseus was the victor. Wherever he went, he freed the people from fear of the evil giants who ruled their lands, and so won their love and gratitude.

At last he came to Athens to the court of King Aegeus, who was under the power of the enchantress Medea. She knew, before the King did, who Theseus was, and she knew the hero would overcome her unless she did away with him first. Pretending friendship, she offered him a cup of wine which contained a death-dealing poison. But Theseus saw that, in spite of her beauty, her eyes were like the eyes of a snake; so he asked her to drink first from the cup. She turned pale, saying that she was ill and could drink no wine. Then he looked into those snake-like eyes and cried, "Drink the wine or die!" and he lifted up his sword to strike her.

She shrieked and dropped the cup. As the wine fell upon the marble pavement, the stone bubbled and hissed and crumbled in the poison, and a poor dog, upon whom it also fell, died instantly. So, mounted on her magic dragon-car, Medea fled and never returned.

When Aegeus saw the sword of Theseus, he knew that this was his son. His joy was great, for now he knew that the kingship would fall on worthy shoulders.

One day Theseus saw that all the people of Athens were weeping with a great grief. He asked his father the cause of it and was told that on this day the dreadful tribute was to be sent to King Minos of Crete. Since conquering Athens, Minos had demanded that the Athenians pay a yearly tribute of seven youths and seven maidens to serve as food for the Minotaur, the monster that had a man's body but the head of a bull and the teeth of a lion. It was kept in Minos' palace, in a labyrinth of such winding passages that, once in the center, no man could find his way out again and was doomed to be destroyed and devoured by the Minotaur.

The ship which was to carry the unhappy youths and maidens to their doom was in the harbor, with its black sails spread. All the friends and relatives of the young people of the city had gathered in a crowd for the drawing of lots that would decide who the victims were to be. Insisting on going as one of the youths, Theseus promised to slay the Minotaur. His father protested but could not influence him. Should Theseus prevail and all was well, the King made Theseus promise to hoist white sails on the ship for the return home.

When the ship reached Knossos, the young men and women were brought into the presence of the King. Theseus told Minos who he was and asked to be allowed to be the first to enter the labyrinth. The King agreed.

Ariadne, the daughter of Minos, saw Theseus and fell in love with his courage. She approached him secretly and gave him a sword and a ball of thread. She made him promise to take her away from Crete if he should succeed in killing the Minotaur.

Theseus entered the labyrinth and proceeded, as he went, unwinding the thread which he had fastened to a stone at the entrance. Prowling the passageways, the Minotaur came upon Theseus, roared like a lion, and charged toward the hero. Theseus slipped away from the monster and let it charge past, then attacked it from behind to strike it dead. Then he found his way out of the labyrinth by following the thread.

Taking Ariadne with them, Theseus and the joyful Athenians sailed away from Crete in the night, but, in their haste and enthusiasm, they forgot to change out the sails to white. Old Aegeus, watching the seas anxiously, saw the ship at last, but with its black sails, and in his grief he dove into the sea. Since then it has been called the Aegean Sea.

Theseus was crowned King of Athens. He was the king who did the most for Athens in this very early time. Through his heroic deeds of the past, in slaying the giants, and through his having freed Athens from paying tribute to King Minos, he had earned the gratitude of many scattered peoples and was able to unite them all into one state, Attica, under the leadership of Athens.

The Aegean Heroes

As civilization moved from the East toward the West, a new time was born. The wisdom of the East, wherein the priests and priest-kings had been the leaders of the people, was forgotten little by little. Having discovered the beauties of the earth, mankind was getting ready to live in the light of his own thinking. Between the old age and the new was the time of heroes, men who overcame monsters and evil giants. By their mighty deeds the heroes showed men how to be brave and true to their word. These heroes became the new leaders of the people who lived around the Aegean Sea.

In the Plain of Argos, at Mycenae and Sparta, at Tiryns near the sea, and in Athens rose massive fortresses with heavy stone foundations and walls. Some of these were built on hills in sight of the sea, the better to protect the huts of the shepherds and gardeners outside the walls, who were dependent on the protection of the princes or kings whose palaces were within. Further to the west and northward was Ithaca, whose king joined the Aegeans in their deeds of courage.

To the East, across the Aegean Sea, was the city of Troy, the greatest of the cities of men. Its walls were so strong and so high that enemies could not scale them or break through them. Troy had high towers and great gates. In its citadels were strong men, well armed. In its treasuries were stores of gold and silver.

Each Western city had its king: Agamemnon, King of Mycenae, was a mighty man and brave. He was a head taller than all the other heroes. His brother, Menelaus, was King of Sparta. Odysseus, King of Ithaca, was the wisest of the kings in the West. The King of Troy was Priam. He was an old man but had sons who were good captains, and the noblest of them was Hector, the Protector of Troy. Another of Priam's sons was not counted among the captains. Paris was his name.

When Paris was a baby, a fortune teller had told Priam that this son would bring trouble upon Troy. So Priam sent Paris away from the city to be brought up by country people as a shepherd.

Now it happened that all the gods were invited to the marriage of Peleus, another hero king, to Thetis, a river nymph. All the goddesses were invited, all except Eris, or Discord, who came uninvited. After the wedding there were games, and Eris threw, among the guests, a golden apple on which were written the words, "For the fairest."

Three goddesses began to quarrel over who should have the apple, each thinking herself the fairest: Aphrodite, Athena and Hera. But no one dared judge who was the fairest until the shepherd, Paris, came by and the guests asked him to be the judge.

Hera said, "If you will give me the apple, I will make you a king."

Athena said, "If you give it to me, I will make you the wisest of men."

Aphrodite said, "I will make you beautiful, and the fairest woman in the world will be your wife."

Paris looked on Aphrodite, and in his eyes she was the fairest, so he gave the apple to her and she was forever afterwards his friend.

Then Paris became the most beautiful of all youths. He traveled through Greece till he came to Sparta where ruled King Menelaus whose Queen Helen was the fairest woman in all the world. Paris fell in love with her, and Aphrodite inspired Helen to fall in love with Paris, who then carried her off to Troy.

King Menelaus sent to Troy demanding that Helen be returned to him. King Priam and Hector knew that a wrong had been done and that Helen should be sent back; but in the council of Troy were vain men who thought it would be a proud boast to be able to say that the fairest woman in all the world was in their city, and they prevailed against Priam and Hector by saying that no little Greek king could make them give her up.

When Agamemnon, King of Mycenae, heard that Troy refused to give up his brother's wife, he vowed to punish Troy. He called all the princes and kings of Greece together and urged them to unite and sail against Troy, take the city, and avenge the injury done to Menelaus. He promised them great glory and riches for themselves.

The kings of Greece took note of their own strength and were eager to make war upon Troy, so they bound themselves by a vow to take the city. Then Agamemnon sent messages to the heroes whose lands were far away—to Odysseus of Ithaca, to Achilles, son of Peleus, and many others—and bid them also enter the war. Within two years, the ships of all the kings and princes were gathered together with their leaders, Agamemnon, Odysseus and Achilles, and they sailed for the coast of Troy.

It was many years before they returned to Greece, and of their leaders, many never returned. Although they captured many cities around Troy, they could not easily conquer Troy itself, for its high walls protected it. For many years the Greeks besieged the city. They built their camp on the seashore, below the walls of Troy, and they built a wall to protect the camp and their ships which were pulled up on the beach. Though the Trojans were safe behind their mighty walls, still they were unable to come and go, nor could they drive away the hosts of the Greeks.

Achilles, son of Peleus (who was the son of Aeacus, a son of Zeus) and Thetis (a sea nymph), had brought with him to the war his special warrior host, the Myrmidons. He also had the two immortal horses given to Peleus by Zeus. Achilles carried a great spear (given to Peleus by Chiron), which none but he could wield. Achilles was the mightiest of the Greek warriors when he deigned to fight; but he was also stubborn and would sometimes fight and sometimes not.

Among the Trojans, Hector alone had the greatness of leadership. Besides being brave, Hector was generous and gentle-spoken to all and thought of his people before himself. After years of the Greeks' siege, Hector decided to take his army outside the city to fight upon the plain and drive the Greeks back to their ships.

Just at this time, Achilles and Agamemnon quarreled over the love of the maiden Briseis. Indeed, Achilles would have killed Agamemnon in anger if the goddess Athena had not intervened. Now Achilles refused to fight, but Hector and the Trojans were encamped on the plain, prepared for battle. Still Achilles refused to fight. When Agamemnon led the battle to the walls of Troy, he was wounded. Hector waited until Agamemnon turned back, then led an attack and would have reached the Greek wall, but Odysseus led a counter-attack and drove the Trojans back.

And so the battle raged back and forth, night and day. Many heroes were wounded. Hector was hurt by a big stone but was revived by the god Apollo.

In the midst of the battle an Eagle and a blood-red Serpent struggled overhead. The Trojans finally broke through the big gate of the Greek wall and rushed to set fire to the Greek ships. Once more the Greeks fought them back and off.

Still Achilles refused to fight, and his dearest friend Patroklos, who had been as a brother to Achilles all his life, persuaded him to let him enter the battle dressed in Achilles' armor and lead Achilles' warriors in the chariot drawn by the two immortal horses. Patroklos inspired courage to the Greeks and, with the Myrmidons, drove the Trojans back to the walls of their city.

Then, Patroklos was hit in the back by a stone. Some say it was Apollo who hurled the stone to bring Patroklos down, and that Apollo did it because he did not want Troy to be taken in this way. As Patroklos lay stunned, Hector slew him and took Achilles' armor for himself.

When Iris, the goddess of the rainbow, informed Achilles of Patroklos' death, Achilles finally agreed to fight. He showed himself without his armor on the Greek wall and shouted so that the Trojans heard him and saw him with a flame of fire around his head. They were afraid and stood still; in that way the Greeks were able to retrieve the body of Patroklos and take him back to their camp, where Achilles grieved bitterly for his lost friend.

Thetis, the mother of Achilles, had Hephaestus make her son a new suit of armor. Wearing this shining armor, Achilles entered the battle to avenge Patroklos. He knew that he too would lose his life. Would not the armor protect him? This would not happen, for when Achilles was only a baby, Thetis had sought to make him immortal through the waters of the River Styx, the sacred river in the underworld which must be crossed by the souls of the dead on their way to the realm of Hades. She had held him by his heel as she dipped him headfirst into the river. Only his heel was untouched and therefore vulnerable.

One cannot tell of the courage of the mortal heroes in this dire struggle without telling of the deeds of the gods. Some of the fateful events were brought to pass by men and unchallenged by the gods, while others took place through the intervention of gods and goddesses. On the side of the Greeks, Athena intervened in the quarrel between Achilles and Agamemnon. Apollo fought for the Trojans by assisting Hector. Aphrodite rescued Paris from the arrow of Menelaus. Athena guided the spear of the Greek warrior Diomedes to kill a

Trojan. Then Aphrodite shielded her son Aeneas, a Trojan, from Diomedes but received a spear wound herself. "The blood of the gods flowed!" and Aphrodite fled. Apollo took her place and carried Aeneas to safety. Ares, the god of war, opposed Diomedes, but Athena mounted the chariot of Diomedes and drove it at Ares, and then guided Diomedes' spear directly and straight into Ares' belly. With a roar as of ten thousand men, Ares flew to Zeus.

Now Zeus commanded the gods to quit their interference, not to help either the Greeks or the Trojans. He himself took charge of the course of the war.

In the end, both Hector and Achilles died in battle. Achilles knew just where to strike Hector who was wearing Achilles' armor. Achilles knew where there was one small opening in that armor and the point of his spear found it, in Hector's neck. But it was the god, Apollo, who knew where to strike Achilles. In spite of Zeus, Apollo guided an arrow shot by Paris into Achilles' heel, and thus delivered the fatal wound.

More than nine years of war had not brought victory to the Greeks or the Trojans. How much longer was the war to rage? The Trojans had received the aid of most of the gods and goddesses, and the Greeks were helped mainly by Athena, the goddess of wisdom. Yet it was Odysseus, wise in himself, who contrived the trick that at the last led to the downfall of Troy.

One morning, when the Trojans looked down from their high walls, they saw no Greek camp, no Greek ships—the Greeks had disappeared. On the empty battle field stood a tremendous wooden horse, and after a time the Trojans went forth to take a closer look. Made of planks, the horse carried writing on it, which said: "The Greeks leave this as an offering to Athena."

Now there was much dispute among the Trojans. Some wanted to push the horse back into the sea. Others wanted to take it as a trophy into the city to Athena's temple. Laocoön, a priest of Troy, insisted that the horse was a trick, that it concealed Greek soldiers. Helen of Sparta, over whom the war had started, walked around the horse calling to each Greek hero in the voice of his wife, but there was only silence. Laocoön hurled a spear into the side of the horse, but there was only a hollow sound as of an empty cavern. Then a terrible thing happened. Two great sea snakes appeared from out of the waves and wrapped themselves around Laocoön and his young two sons. Tightening their coils, the snakes crushed the lives out of the three. Then the snakes made their way to Athena's temple and vanished.

The Trojans believed that Laocoön had been punished by Athena for his offense to the goddess. So sure were they that they made a breach in the walls of Troy so as to take the great horse into the city.

That night there was feasting and merriment among the Trojans, and at last they fell asleep without fear of an enemy presence in their midst. In the silence of the sleeping city, an opening appeared in the side of the horse and from it emerged Odysseus, who had designed the whole plan, and he was followed by numbers of Greeks. A beacon fire was lighted and answered by a flare from Agamemnon's ship as it led the other Greek ships out of hiding back to the beaches below Troy.

Before the citizens of Troy awakened, the streets were swarming with Greeks. They set fire to the houses and sought out men, women and children to slay them. King Priam was shown no mercy, Hector's infant son was thrown from the walls of Troy, and Menelaus sought out Helen to kill her, but her beauty overcame him, and he took her captive, eventually, back to Sparta. Troy was reduced to ashes, its people either slaughtered or taken as slaves.

Athena's wrath was great when one of her priestesses was dragged from the altar in the temple. The goddess vowed unhappy fates for the Greek leaders, Menelaus, Agamemnon and Odysseus, and called upon Poseidon to help her. Nevertheless, the Trojan War was ended. Later a poet called Homer wrote the whole story down in *The Iliad*.

Heinrich Schliemann

Heinrich Schliemann was born in 1822, many centuries after the fall of Troy. He was the son of a German pastor, who told him all the old Greek tales, including the story of the Trojan War.

As a boy, Heinrich lived in a romantic neighborhood. Behind his father's garden was a pool from which, it was said, a maiden rose holding a silver bowl in her hand. Similar tales were told in connection with neighboring hills and forests.

At age fourteen Heinrich had to go to work as an errand boy for a country grocer. One evening a man came into the shop and asked for some refreshment, then sat down and began to recite Greek poetry. Heinrich couldn't understand Greek, but the melodious words stirred him deeply, and he asked the man to say them again and again. After that Heinrich's deepest desire was to learn Greek.

A few years later he went to work as an errand boy in a business house in Amsterdam. Wherever he went, even in the rain, he carried a book of Homer with him, reading and memorizing passage after passage.

Schliemann did well. Soon he had a business of his own, and at last he had time to learn Greek. He read everything he could find about the ancient Greeks. He believed that the tales of Troy were true although everyone laughed at such an idea. He even dreamed in his sleep of the place where he would find the ruins of Troy.

In 1870, as soon as he had accumulated enough money to finance an expedition, he went to that place and there found nine cities, buried one on top of the other. Later archaeologists discovered that the sixth city was the Troy of Homer's *Iliad*.

One of the books that Schliemann had read was by Pausanias, an ancient Greek traveler who described Mycenae and the tomb of Agamemnon. Seeking the truth of the legend, Schliemann went to Mycenae and there found, in the depths of the earth, not only a gorgeous and princely tomb but also the ruins of a great, fortified palace such as had been described in *The Iliad*. The tomb showed that the king had been buried in great magnificence. A golden crown, diadems, pendants, necklaces, ornaments, and plates and vases of pure gold were piled high in the tomb. In another tomb he found 870 objects made of the purest gold. Heinrich thought he had found Agamemnon's tomb. But later research revealed this was not true; rather the tomb was from a period several hundred years before the time of Menelaus.

The Twelve Labors of Heracles

Heracles was the son of Zeus and Alcmene, a mortal princess. Out of jealousy, Hera sent two snakes to kill the child, but the boy strangled them. Hera decided that she couldn't succeed in taking his life, so she made Zeus decree that Heracles should be a slave and serve his cousin Eurystheus, King of Tiryns, for a certain number of years.

While he was growing up, Heracles was educated by Chiron, a wise and good centaur, who taught him how to use all weapons, how to wrestle and master all others in a fight, and how to master himself. The day came when Hermes appeared and told Heracles that he must go to serve Eurystheus, who required him to perform ten great labors before he could again be free.

THE NEMEAN LION

An enormous lion had its den in the Nemean Forest. All people lived in fear, for the beast gave them no peace, by carrying them off to devour them and by carrying off their cattle and sheep as well. No one dared to fight the lion. Heracles was sent out to find and destroy it. People warned him not to attempt it, but without fear he tracked the lion down and slew it. Ever after he wore the lion's pelt as a cloak.

THE HYDRA OF LERNA

In the marshes of Lerna lurked a seven-headed serpent, the Hydra, which devoured men and beasts, and because of its poisonous breath, men who came near her sickened and died. Armed with a great sword, Heracles attacked the serpent and cut off one of its heads, but seven new heads sprang out to take the place of the one. Heracles fought on, and as he cut off more heads, he seared each stump with a flaming firebrand and so destroyed the Hydra. Knowing that thereafter his arrows would inflict fatal wounds, he dipped his arrows in its poisonous blood.

THE STAG OF CERYNEA

The third labor of Heracles was to chase and capture a golden-horned, brazen-footed stag which ran so fleetly that its feet barely touched the ground. Heracles finally caught the stag in one of the lands in the far north by driving it into a huge snowdrift.

THE ERYMANTHIAN BOAR

His fourth labor was to bring back alive a wild boar that haunted the mountain of Erymanthus. Heracles captured the boar and brought it back to Eurystheus, who was so afraid of the boar that he asked Heracles to take it away and dispose of it.

THE AUGEAN STABLES

Next Heracles was sent out to clean, in a single day, the immense stables where King Augeas kept a herd of over a thousand cattle. As the stables hadn't been cleaned for over thirty years, the job seemed impossible. Heracles found a river flowing nearby and turned it from its course to flow through the stables and wash out the filth. Then he returned the river to its original course.

THE STYMPHALIAN BIRDS

For the sixth labor, Heracles was sent to put an end to a dangerous and awful brood of man-eating birds with bronze beaks and metal feathers that could slice up anyone who came near them. Their guano (bird feces) was poisonous and created deadly fumes, so Heracles could not venture into the birds' swamp to slay them. Athena took pity on Heracles and had Hephaestus make a special rattle. When Heracles shook the rattle, the birds were terrified and flew into the air. Heracles shot most of them with his poison arrows; the rest flew far away, never to return.

THE CRETAN BULL

The beautiful bull given to King Minos of Crete by Poseidon, god of seas and rivers, was to be offered as a sacrifice to the gods. But Minos had kept the bull and sacrificed another. Angry, Poseidon maddened the bull which rushed about wildly killing and destroying crops and all who came its way. Heracles caught it and bound it. He brought it to Eurystheus, who, fearful once more, hid in a large jar and wanted to sacrifice the bull to Athena. When Athena refused, the bull was released to wander away.

THE MARES OF DIOMEDES

Diomedes, King of Thrace, kept some fine horses which he fed on human flesh. He would capture and kill all strangers to feed to his mares, which made them quite wild. Heracles captured the stable and fed Diomedes' body to his own horses. Then he bound the horses' mouths and sent them to Eurystheus. The horses became calm and acted like normal mares once they stopped eating people.

THE BELT OF HIPPOLYTE

Hippolyte, Queen of the Amazons, had a beautiful, jeweled girdle. King Eurystheus' vain daughter wanted this girdle, so Heracles was sent to get it. He presented himself to Queen Hippolyte and told her what he wanted. Impressed by his reputation, she probably would have given him the belt, had not Hera, disguised as an Amazon, spread a false rumor among the other Amazons that Heracles really had come to kidnap their Queen. So they flew to arms! Heracles fought them single-handedly, killed Hippolyte, won the girdle, and brought it back to the princess, the daughter of Eurystheus.

THE CATTLE OF GERYONES

Next, Heracles was sent to capture a herd of divine cattle belonging to the giant Geryones, who lived in Erythea. When Heracles was on his way home with this beautiful herd, another giant stole some of the cows. Heracles forced his way into the giant's cave, attacked and killed him, and then took all the cattle back to Eurystheus.

Still, the King was not satisfied. He gave Heracles two more tasks because Eurystheus said two of the ten completed labors didn't really count.

THE HESPERIAN APPLES

The golden apples of the Hesperides, daughters of Hesperus (god of the West Wind), had been entrusted to them by Hera. The apples had been a wedding present for Hera. Heracles was sent to get them, but he didn't even know where to find the Hesperides. After making numerous journeys, he discovered that the daughters had carried the apples off to Africa, hung them on a tree, and set a dragon to guard them night and day. Heracles still didn't know what part of Africa. Wherever he went, he questioned nymphs and gods, and finally went up to the mountain where Prometheus, a son of the Titan Iapetus, was chained and still suffering as he had for long ages. Heracles freed Prometheus who, in gratitude, told Heracles where the apples would be found.

Finally Heracles found Atlas, who supported the heavens on his broad shoulders. Heracles took his place and held up the sky while Atlas went to get the apples. When Atlas returned with the apples, he tried to persuade Heracles to keep holding up the heavens while he would take the apples to Eurystheus. Heracles agreed, but asked Atlas to hold the heavens for a moment while he put a cushion on his shoulders. Thus Heracles tricked Atlas back to his burden and took the apples himself to Eurystheus.

CERBERUS

For the twelfth and final task, Heracles was sent to capture Cerberus, the fearful, three-headed dog which guarded the gates to the underworld. Heracles overpowered Cerberus with his bare hands and slung the beast over his back. He brought Cerberus to Eurystheus who, when he saw the dog, was so afraid that, again, he hid in a big jar and refused to come out until Heracles returned the dog to the underworld.

His twelve labors completed, Heracles was now a free man. Surely the path to freedom for every man is to carry out life's tasks, however hard they may be. There are many other stories about the life of Heracles, and when he died, Zeus came down from Mount Olympus and carried his soul up to live with the gods and with beautiful Hebe, the goddess of youth, as his bride.

The Olympic Games

After Heracles completed his twelve labors, he journeyed to Olympia to the Oracle of Zeus. He called together the young men from all parts of Greece and invited them to show their skill in various games. He himself took part and inspired them to show great strength, speed and grace. Thereafter, these games were celebrated every fifth year, and the Greeks measured their time in olympiads (five-year periods) instead of in years. The first games were officially recorded in 776 BC, but Homer describes them also in *The Iliad* and *The Odyssey*.

The games were held in August or September and lasted five days, during which time all warfare had to stop and all ordinary business. For people who journeyed from all parts of Greece to and from Olympia, all roads were declared safe, and anyone who dared attack travelers was punished.

Visitors thronged every road and came not only from all Greece but from the far-off colonies in Asia; clad in rich robes, they brought an oriental splendor in their trains. Others came from Italy to the west, and other dark and warm-blooded men came up from Africa. There were rich men on camels and horses, accompanied by their slaves who brought everything for their masters' comforts. There were poor men who tramped on foot, who forgot their tired feet in thinking of the joys of the games to come.

Merchants came with rich and rare goods to sell, and there were sculptors bearing statues for the temples, poets wanting to recite their poems, musicians playing their instruments, and gymnastics teachers coming to learn something new for their teaching. The women were left at home; it was too long and hard a journey, and too public an occasion for them.

But one year some women from Sparta came to compete in the games. They beat some of the men and won several events. After that, all women were banned from the games.

There was no city at Olympia, only fields and stadiums for competition and the temples, among them the great temple of Zeus, which housed the marvelous statue of the god sculpted of gold and ivory by Phidias, a statue that became one of the Seven Wonders of the Ancient World. The Greeks liked to say, "Anyone standing in front of this statue forgets all his troubles and is filled with joy." People set up tents for shelter and booths for the merchants. All around, a great camp arose where friends met to talk over all that had happened to them since last they met. Public announcements were made by heralds regarding the affairs between the various city-states: wars, treaties, new colonies.

All the athletes arrived at Olympia for special training thirty days before the games. Taking special training, only men of pure Greek blood could compete. No one guilty of any crime or of disrespect to the gods could enter the games. Each candidate had to prove that he had had ten months of training before coming to Olympia. Names of the candidates were written on a white board, and should a man withdraw after his name was posted, he was branded a coward. A boar was then sacrificed to Zeus while each athlete took an oath that he was a full Greek citizen and that he would follow all the rules of the contest and play fair. In more than a thousand years, only six or seven names of competitors were found guilty of breaking their oaths.

On the first day of the games, the contestants made sacrifices and held processions in which appeared, riding in chariots and bearing costly gifts to place in the temple, the representatives of the different city-states. The actual contests took place on the next three days in the great stadium where every seat was filled, and the surrounding hills were crowded with spectators who brought their food with them and sat from sunrise to sunset for fear of losing their places. The bright sun shone on bare heads, for Zeus was present everywhere, and no one dared enter his presence with a covered head.

The contests on the first day included foot races of 200 yards to three miles in distance, and the pentathlon which consisted of five different events: the discus throw, javelin throwing, running, jumping and wrestling. The same competitors took part in all of them. The winner had to win three out of the five contests. The judges paid special attention to the gracefulness of every movement. The discus and spear throwing were usually accompanied by flute music.

On the second day, and most exciting of all, were the four-horsed chariot races. According to Homer, "The charioteers all together lifted the lash above their steeds and smote them with the reins and called on them eagerly with words, and they forthwith sped swiftly over the plain, with the rising dust like a cloud or whirlwind beneath their breasts, and their manes waved on the blowing wind. The chariots ran sometimes on the bounteous earth, and other times they would bound into the air. The drivers stood in the cars, and the heart in every man beat with desire for victory, and they called every man to his horses that flew amid their dust across the plain."

After a night of feasting and celebration, the third day of the Olympics began with the very solemn sacrifice to Zeus. The rest of the day was devoted to events for boys over 17 but under 20; these events were similar to those for older athletes: the stade race and *pankration*, a combination of boxing and wrestling. Last of all, on the fourth day of the games, came the roughest and fiercest of all the contests, the boxing and wrestling matches.

The fifth day was for the awarding of prizes. They were very simple but more highly valued than rich gifts. The prizes were olive wreaths cut from a sacred olive tree by a boy with a golden knife, a boy especially chosen. Both of his parents had to be alive. The wreaths were placed on a table in sight of all the people. A herald announced the name of the victor, his father's name, and the city from which he came. Then one of the judges placed the wreath on his head. This was the proudest moment of his life! After the awards were acknowledged, sacrifices were made to Zeus, followed by feasting, which lasted late into the night. Every kind of honor was shown the victors: Poets wrote odes about them. Sculptors made statues of them, for every athlete who had won three victories was honored by having his statue placed in the open space outside the temple of Zeus.

A victor was proud, too, of the honor he brought to his native city, and upon his return, the city would declare a public holiday. The people sang songs of triumph to greet him. The road he was led on to his father's house was strewn with flowers. In Athens, the victors were allowed to dine at public expense in the places where the counselors and great men of the city took their meals.

Inspired by the idea that athletic training gave beauty, grace, and strength to the human body, the Greeks considered that to run gracefully was as important as to run swiftly, and so they did not keep records of who ran more swiftly or who threw the discus the furthest. Pindar, the Greek poet, put these words into a song about the Olympic victors: "He that overcometh hath, because of the games, a sweet tranquility throughout his life forever more."

The Delphic Oracle

Few stories of ancient Greece can be told without hearing about the Oracles. At certain places, far from the dwellings of men, there were shrines where people could go and ask the guidance of the gods, and receive their advice through the priests or priestesses who served the gods in these shrines or Oracles.

The greatest Oracle in all of Greece was the Oracle of Apollo at Delphi. The Greeks tell a story of a great deluge after which the surface of the earth remained covered with slime and muddy water. Out of the slime was born a monster serpent, the Python, who brought fear and death to the race of men. None dared approach the Python to slay it but, from his sun-chariot in the sky, Apollo heard the prayers from men for deliverance from the serpent. Fearlessly, Apollo approached the horrible being and slew it with his golden arrows. Then he chose the place where he had slain the Python as a place where he could dwell, at times, to make his will known to men. This was at Delphi.

A temple of Apollo was then built under the rocky cliffs of Mount Parnassus. Within the temple dwelt a priestess-prophetess, the Pythoness, who served Apollo and sought his answers to the questions that were asked by the people for many generations. When people came asking the god for help and advice, the Pythoness would present the question to Apollo. A misty vapor would rise from a cleft in the rock floor and surround the priestess while the god, Apollo, spoke; she, in turn, would speak his answers to the questions.

Through this Oracle, Apollo played a great part in the affairs of the Greeks and of other peoples, sometimes giving straightforward answers, sometimes riddles that had to be pondered for the right meaning. On the wall of the Delphic shrine were carved two such riddles: "Know thyself" and "Nothing in excess."

The Hand of Greece

Greece is a land of islands, sea, and mountains. Deep bays and gulfs wash between the fingers of land that reach out into the Aegean Sea. One can count five fingers on this hand of land that seems to be reaching out toward the East as if to receive its gifts. The Gulf of Corinth, almost cutting the peninsula in two, brings the sea into the midst of the mountains. And these mountains and islands divided ancient Greece in such a way that many separate city-states developed.

The Aegean hero-kings who overthrew Troy were gradually supplanted by invading nomads, first the Achaeans from the west, later the Dorians from the north. Over a period of three hundred years, these peoples took possession of the Greek Peninsula, of all the Aegean islands, and of Crete. This mixture of peoples—Aegeans, Achaeans and Dorians—became the Greek people. Their cities developed along the coasts and, of course, they became a seafaring people.

From the earliest times, when herdsmen (tent dwellers wearing sheepskin coats and driving cattle and sheep) wandered into the "hand" of Greece, the head man of each family had the power of life or death over those who belonged to the family, and each family was independent in itself.

As they settled in small villages around which they began to cultivate the land as well as raise cattle, several families would group together as *phratiae* (clans). Then groups of phratiae would combine as small kingdoms to serve and be protected by a king. The people lived side by side around the king's fortress, and a city would grow to be ruled by the king. When he died, his son became king in his place. Although the king was usually thought of as one of the gods, he could govern the people only with the consent of a council of the leading men, and they were usually chosen by the people because they were good warriors and leaders.

Whether they were councilmen or not, all the men of a city would be called together to hear what the king and his council had decided on and to give their approval. This gathering was called the "assembly." Thus was a city governed, and thus it also governed the surrounding country as a city-state. Each city-state or kingdom had its own form of government.

Of all the city-states of Greece, two played leading roles in Greek history: Sparta and Athens. They governed themselves as differently as two unlike individuals. In Sparta the citizens were expected to serve the state, in Athens the state sought to serve its citizens. And their first leaders, two very different individuals, were Lycurgus of Sparta and Solon of Athens.

Lycurgus of Sparta (9th century BC)

Sparta, the one-time kingdom of Menelaus, was taken over by invaders. Having grown as a city out of a group of villages, Sparta had no fortress. A wise man of Sparta was asked whether or not a wall should be built around the city. He answered, "The city is well-fortified which hath a wall of men instead of bricks." This wise man was Lycurgus, the brother of a Spartan king who died leaving a young child as his heir. Lycurgus offered to rule so long as the king's son was too young. Many disbelieved Lycurgus and plotted against his life, so he left Sparta to visit Crete and Asia Minor.

In Crete, people were sober and temperate, leading simple lives. In Asia Minor there was much wealth, comfort and pleasure-seeking. Lycurgus decided that wealth did not bring happiness nor were the rich states the best governed.

The Spartans missed him and called him back. He went home believing that a simple life was better achieved by a nation of warriors who would be disciplined and selfless, and that each citizen was born not to please himself in life but to serve his state. He intended to establish certain laws to bring about a nation to support this kind of life. Before going to Sparta, he visited a special place. He went to Delphi to consult the Priestess and receive the guidance of Apollo. There he was told that his prayers had been heard, and the city that observed his laws would be the most famous in all the world. Lycurgus did not become the King but rather he was the Law-Giver of Sparta.

When he returned to Sparta, he found some Spartans rich and others poor. He decreed that all should share wealth equally, and he divided land into lots, giving each citizen an equal share. Having recalled all the gold and silver coins, he gave out huge iron coins instead. This money had little value as it was heavy and hard to handle. No one hoarded it and no one could buy luxuries from the East, as no traders came to Sparta for iron money.

Lycurgus forbade most Spartans to travel lest they see the luxuries he had seen and prefer them to the simple life. Each householder was to make and build what he needed for living by using only the simplest of tools, the ax and saw. Houses and furniture, thus, were roughly and simply constructed, and laws governed what the Spartans could eat, which was only certain simple, healthy foods.

The citizen of Sparta was he who lived in the city. Outside the city lived the free men, subjects of the Spartan kings. The Aegeans, who had been conquered by the invaders, were the slaves of the Spartans. They were called helots. There were two kings, succeeded always by their sons. The kings led the armies, sat in seats of honor, were given double portions of food, and had bodyguards of the best soldiers. The Council which governed was made up of the two kings and twenty-eight other men over sixty years of age, the senators, who were elected for life.

These elections took place in locked rooms, where scribes listened and wrote down the extent of the shouts of the citizens outside as the candidates appeared before them. The most shouting, of course, signaled the winner, who was then garlanded and led in a procession to the temple to thank the gods. All men who were citizens of Sparta and over thirty years old became members of the assembly. The assembly could reject the decisions of the council as to war or peace; but members of the assembly were not permitted to take part in the discussions of the council. It was the assembly that elected the senators. Women could not be citizens or participate in government.

Every Spartan had to be ready at any minute to fight well for his city. The helots did all the work of farming, building and herding, while the Spartan warriors gave all their time to soldiering, to becoming good bricks in the "wall of men" which protected the city.

Education in Sparta

The childhood and schooling of a warrior-class Spartan was already the beginning of soldiering. A newborn boy was judged by the Elders of the city as to whether he or she looked strong and healthy enough to be allowed to live. The baby's first bath was in wine, to increase strength. The first teachers were, in infancy, the Spartan nurses who trained the children's bodies through vigorous exercise, who made them eat the food set before them, who taught them to be brave in the dark or when left alone, and who demanded that they be in good humor at all times with no whining, fretting or shows of bad temper.

At seven years old, the children left home and went to a school like an army camp. The boys went to one barracks and the girls to another. Each boy was enrolled in a company wherein the older boy with the most courage was the captain and gave orders to be obeyed. The girls had a similar arrangement.

The pupils in the Spartan schools had to learn the following: perfect obedience, as, for instance, to walk through the streets with hands inside the folds of one's cloak and eyes fixed on the ground, and in silence; to endure pain; to win contests in running, jumping, wrestling and boxing; to take hardship: being allowed only one coat a year, having to make their own beds from rushes which they had to get from a river's edge, and accepting a very small food allowance so they would learn to steal their food or go without. The boys were required to learn only enough reading and writing to honor the gods and to serve their needs as soldiers. The only music they trained in were battle songs and prayers to the gods. The girls were trained in all the Spartan athletics and learned how to run a household and manage slaves. They also learned needlecraft, to read and write as well as the boys, and to dance and sing to honor the gods.

Older men and women were always around watching to see if the children were fit to become Spartan warriors or mothers of warriors and punishing them if they failed in any task. If children were caught in the act of stealing, they were whipped, not for stealing but for allowing themselves to be caught. Older boys were often whipped publicly before the altar of Artemis so they would learn to endure pain without crying out.

Every evening the captains called the boys together before the older officers, and the girls were called before the heads of their schools. Questions were asked such as, "Who is the best man in the city?" or "What do you think of such and such an action?" This was to teach judgment, and the answers had to include reasons in as few words as possible. Boys who could not do this well had their thumbs bitten by their captains. Girls were expected to develop the same level of judgment to be able to parent their families.

A Spartan man was allowed to marry at the age of twenty, but he could not live at home with his wife until he was thirty. He had to do military service and live in the adult male barracks. At thirty he was through with training and became a soldier-citizen and could live at home, but this did not happen often. All men ate in common dining halls or tents to which they contributed their share of barley, cheese, wine and figs. "Men who ate together in peace fought together in war," thought Lycurgus. After the evening meal, the men went home in the dark. No lights were permitted, as Spartans had to be able to march boldly in the dark.

Spartan wives and mothers were educated to be physically strong and ready to sacrifice their husbands and sons for their country. Their farewell as their soldiers left for battle was, "Come home either victorious with your shields or dead on them." This acknowledged that the heavy shield had to be cast aside if a Spartan was fleeing from an enemy—a disgrace! If killed in battle, the soldier was carried home on his shield.

In time of war, the soldiers dressed in fine clothes and costly armor, their hair curled. They marched to battle to the sound of music. A Greek historian wrote, "It was a magnificent and terrible sight to see them march to the tune of their flutes, without any disorder in their ranks, with untroubled minds and expressionless faces, calmly and cheerfully moving with the music to the deadly fight..."

The Spartan lifestyle came into being through the laws of Lycurgus. Although he felt that the laws and customs were firmly established, he feared that, when he died, they might be changed. He called a special assembly and told the citizens that he had to go to Delphi to consult the Oracle on some matter.

He made the Kings, the Council and the Assembly promise not to change the laws which had been established until he returned.

He went to Delphi, and, again, the Oracle announced that the laws of Lycurgus were such as to make his city very famous. Lycurgus sent this oracle in writing to Sparta. He offered up a sacrifice to Apollo at Delphi, then ended his own life, thus making sure that the Spartans would keep his laws, according to their promise, forever.

Lycurgus had done his work well. The system he established lasted many years and produced the greatest warriors of the ancient world.

Earliest Athens

Athens was the most beautiful city in Greece. Near the sea stretched a plain, surrounded toward the east by hills where lived the wild goats. The hills were purple with thyme and filled with the murmur of bees. To the north loomed a great mountain famous for its shining white marble which gleamed rosy red when the sun went down.

Rising out of the plain was a great, oval-shaped rock, on top of which stood the Acropolis, the center of the city. In ancient times it was the king's fortress, but later it was transformed into a group of temples to the deities. The largest was the temple of Athena, the Parthenon.

From the Acropolis the land sloped gently to the sea. The plain was watered by the River Cephisus, the only stream in Attica which did not run dry in the summertime. On its banks were groves of olive trees, giving a touch of dark grey-green to the landscape. In the center of the plain, at the foot of the Acropolis, was Athens.

The Acropolis had very strong walls and there were nine gates before the main entrance. This made it almost impossible for an enemy to take the fortress. Inside the walls was a well, so there was always water for those who defended the Acropolis.

History has told us almost nothing about the mighty men who built the Athenian Acropolis. Only in a legend do we hear that one of the earliest rulers of Athens was a king named Cecrops. All kinds of stories surround his name, and it was believed that he was not altogether human but a being who had grown out of the earth, half-man, half-serpent.

While he was king, the city became so lively and beautiful that the gods watched it with great interest. Two of them, Poseidon and Athena, vied with each other for the city's name. To settle the argument Zeus decreed that the city would have the name of the one who would create the most valuable object for the use of human beings.

So, Poseidon raised his trident and struck the ground with it, and from that ground sprang forth a noble horse. The watchful gods were greatly delighted as Poseidon explained to them the noble qualities of the horse.

Athena, in turn, produced an olive tree. The gods laughed scornfully at the sight of it in comparison with the spirited horse, until she told them of the many uses to which the wood, leaves and fruit could be put and explained that the olive was a sign of peace and prosperity—far more desirable than the horse who represented war and wretchedness. The gods had to agree that her gift was the best, and so the city of Athens was named for her.

Solon of Athens (c. 639–c. 559 BC)

Some two hundred years after Lycurgus lived and died, the Athenian, Solon, played a very important part in the affairs of Athens. His aims and the spirit of his leadership were new in the history of the world.

Like other Greek cities, Athens had been ruled in hereditary monarchy by kings who became kings because they were the sons of kings. These kings had complete power over the army, the religion, and the laws of the state.

Then came a time when the nobles took power away from the kings and gave it to certain of their leaders instead. The nobles elected their best general to take command of the army and placed another man in charge of enforcing all laws. A third man had authority over all religious sacrifices and ceremonies of state. These three were called the *Archons* (rulers), and six additional men were elected to help them rule. Only men from the class of nobles could be elected as Archons, men who were the best educated and most wealthy. This type of government was called an oligarchy (the rule of the few).

Although by reason of their education and experience, the Archons should have been fit to rule the people, they began to covet power and to seek riches beyond what they had. Then came a time of great discontent among the people. There had been wars, the harvests had been bad, and food was so scarce that people were starving. The rich nobles had loaned money to the working class and to farmers. But when war and famine made it impossible for the people to pay their debts, laws were made which forced them to sell the land and later themselves as slaves. When, from hunger, they stole food, they could be punished by death.

The people began to question the justice of their rulers and ask, "What is the difference between a rich man and a poor man, between the noble and the common man, the free man and the slave?" "Why is one better than another?" "Who are citizens and what does it mean to be a citizen?" The more such questions were asked, the more cruel and unjust the rulers became. Conditions became very bad in Athens, and the people said among themselves, "We will not obey forever."

It was at this time that Solon first showed his leadership. He was a noble by birth, but because he was a poor man, he became a merchant. This enabled him to travel in far lands and see the world, and to always be learning something new. He was also a poet, and some verses he composed led to his first fame!

The Island of Salamis was near the harbor of Athens and the city wanted to own it. The neighboring State of Megara, across the gulf, also wished to possess this island, and the two states went to war over it. The war lasted for such a long time and was so costly and unsuccessful for Athens that the Athenians decided to give up the fight. Solon thought this was a disgrace. Knowing many men would be glad to follow a courageous leader, he composed some fiery verses and recited them in the *Agora*, or marketplace. Calling on the Athenians not to be shameful cowards but to press on in the fight for Salamis, his verses were so inspiring that the Athenians decided to try again. This time they won the island.

Solon was held in such high honor now that the nobles asked him to become the Archon concerned with the laws of the city. He consented and so became one of the first great lawmakers of Athens. The first thing he did was to set all debtors free from their debts. Likewise he freed all who were slaves because of debt. This made many of the Athenians so happy that they celebrated the event for many years in a festival called "The Casting off of Burdens."

Solon loved Athens and wanted its people to be justly treated, so he changed the government of the state in such a way that even the poorest citizens could vote in the Assembly. He also made a law that the richer the man, the more tax money he had to pay the state. He set a limit to the amount of land any one person could own, thus preventing anyone from becoming too rich. A most important change that Solon brought about was to put the courts of justice in the hands of the people instead of the nobles. Thus, although the poorer citizens could not become Archons, they could be elected to the courts to serve as judges. Solon also ruled that the Council of Athens should consist of men elected by the Assembly of all the four tribes of Attica; thus these tribes would all be represented in the government.

While the ordinary people benefited from Solon's laws, many of the nobles disliked them. Many quarrels and forceful fights took place before Athens became a limited democracy. Yet Solon was the first one to change the state from being ruled by "the few" to being ruled by "the many."

That Solon was a leader who did not think of himself but only of his people was shown especially by one of his actions. After he had set forth the laws that brought such helpful changes for the people, he decided that they might work better if he himself went away, so he left Greece for ten years. He was called back because some nobles were breaking laws. He returned, straightened things out, and then retired from public life.

The Tyrant, Pisistratus (c. 605–527 BC)

There were still men in Greece who sought power for themselves. Those who succeeded were called tyrants. The most famous tyrant of Athens was Pisistratus. While yet a general in the army, he deceived the people into thinking that his only wish was to serve the state. In reality his one desire was to become the sole ruler of Athens.

To gain his ends he played certain tricks on the Athenians. One day he appeared in the Agora in his chariot. He had had it and himself sprinkled with blood. He appeared to be severely wounded and, when asked what had happened, he exclaimed that his enemies had attacked him. His friends then crowded into a meeting of the Assembly and insisted that he should be voted a bodyguard of fifty men who could protect him from further attack. When this was done, Pisistratus organized the bodyguard and quickly took possession of the Acropolis. But when he tried to become master of the state, he was driven out of Athens.

Pisistratus did not give up. He contrived another trick. This time he chose the event of a great festival and appeared in the midst of the crowds, again in his chariot. At his side stood a tall and beautiful woman dressed like Athena and carrying Athena's shield and spear. The people were fooled; they thought that the goddess had come down from Mount Olympus to show that she favored Pisistratus, so he was received as a ruler but once again was driven out and this time stayed away ten years.

The third time he came back with a strong army of paid soldiers who were successful in seizing the power for him. So he became Tyrant and ruled Athens for ten years before he died.

In spite of all this, Pisistratus did some constructive things while he was Tyrant. He had an aqueduct built to bring water into the city, and he built new roads. Along these roads, near springs and fountains, were placed small statues of Hermes, and on the pedestals were engraved verses to cheer travelers on their way. He made a law that men wounded in battle and the families of those killed should be cared for by the state. He built a new temple for Athena on the Acropolis and another for Dionysos, at the foot of the Acropolis, where early Greek drama was performed. The temple for Zeus which he started was so great that it was never finished in his lifetime. Although he was a good ruler, the people were deprived of the right to govern themselves, and no one opposed him.

After Pisistratus' death, his two sons succeeded him, but they were so disliked that two young Athenians formed a plot to take their lives at the time of a certain festival. The day came, and one son was killed; the other escaped. The two conspirators were seized and put to death. Hippias, the one who escaped, continued to rule Athens. He became more and more cruel and treated his subjects so badly that the people were bowed down under his oppression.

During this time, the Spartans received a very strange command from the Oracle at Delphi. Every time anyone from Sparta went to consult the Oracle on any matter, the answer was always: "First set Athens free." At last, tired of receiving no answers more helpful, Sparta sent an army to Athens and drove out the tyrant Hippias.

Sparta was no friend of democracy. As soon as Hippias was overthrown, the Spartan king, Cleomenes, tried to force another man into power in Athens. A friend of the former tyrant, his name was Isagoras. The Athenians then rose up and fought the Spartans. They blockaded King Cleomenes in the Acropolis, and he was forced to surrender. At last Athens freed herself from the rule of tyrants.

Themistocles and the Persian Wars (c. 525–c. 460 BC)

The sun is shining down brightly upon a great, outdoor square in Athens. This place is the Agora, the meeting place of men. On two sides of the square rise beautiful buildings and temples of white marble. On the other two sides are covered porches where people may stand and walk, sheltered from the sun or from rain and cold winds. The open square is full of people. A lot of them are busily buying and selling at the booths and stalls in one part of the Agora. In the other part many men are walking here and there and talking. Their voices rise and fall, and their movements and gestures are always toward each other.

Their white robes gleam like the marble columns of the buildings. As each man speaks, another listens, then he, in turn speaks, and so, many talk and listen. Altogether the sound is like a great river clashing the rocks together in its course. The Agora is the most important place in Athens because there the spirit that dwelt in each man could speak to other men, each one enjoying what he heard and having something to say in return. Every morning the Agora was full of people, mostly men, who wanted to hear the news of the day, to discuss the affairs of state, to put questions, to give answers. In the market the countrymen and merchants sold their produce to the slaves of different households who did the buying for their masters.

One noonday the men in the Agora were dispersing to go out to the *gymnasia* to watch the young men practice their skills for the Olympian games. A little boy was on his way, with his pedagog, to the Palaestra for instruction in wrestling, discus throwing, jumping and running. A musician played his lyre. Through the Agora wound a procession of men and women. Their slaves were laden with jars, bundles, furnishings, bowls of fruit and grain. It was unusual to see women in the Agora.

The onlookers talked and little Themistocles listened. They said this was a company of Greeks who were leaving Athens and sailing that day across the Aegean Sea to Ionia, there to settle in new homes. The Oracle at Delphi had promised them success in finding good land for wheat, grapes, olives and water. The procession moved toward the Town Hall where the leaders of the expedition would be given a brazier of coals from the sacred fire of Athens with which to light the fires in their new homes.

Many such companies had sailed east toward the mainland of Asia. Greek cities had grown up where people had set up self-governing states, independent of their mother city. Even so, these people looked back to their homeland with affection. Wherever they went, they were still Greeks, speaking Greek and worshiping the Greek gods.

It was nothing new to see such colonists set forth, but Themistocles was filled with wonder. The East! He was old enough to attend to the talk of grownups and wonder at it. From what they said, the East was full of light and wisdom. Many persons from Greece went to the East to learn the wisdom of old. The light of the rising sun, golden yellow in the sky, coloring the east, seemed to Themistocles to be the very Light which men went to find. While to the west, where the blue sea stretched, all was unknown, though some spoke of a lost world sunk below the waters when the gods sent a flood to purify the earth. From the grownups Themistocles had heard that in the north was a land of frost and ice, beyond which lived the Hyperboreans, a race of beings who lived in perfect happiness. To reach them through the white snows was not possible, so great were the dangers. Whiteness to the north, blue to the west, yellow to the east! When Themistocles imagined a color to the south, where the great warmth of the sun flooded the earth—it was red. But it was the East that lured him. Maybe he would go there when he became a man. Little did he know that, when he was a man, the East would come to him.

What kind of a life did Themistocles have as a boy, and what kind of a boy was he? His parents were humble people. His home was on a quiet, dirt street in Athens between the windowless walls of other houses. Only the locked doors of the houses faced the street and behind each one sat the slave whose duty it was to open the door to guests. Inside the house of an Athenian was a courtyard, an atrium, surrounded by the rooms of the house. The sacred fire was always kept burning in the dining hall, but there were no stoves, only pots of coal to warm the rooms in winter. The people slept on beds without springs or sheets. Athenians did not think material possessions were important. They had no clocks, no compasses, no buttons, no electricity, no stockings. They studied poetry without books, geography without maps, politics without newspapers. All private houses were alike, whether of the rich or the poor. The wealth was spent on beautiful public buildings which all could enjoy. In the homes, the rooms were small and dark except for light from the courtyard.

Themistocles' mother stayed at home most of the time overseeing slaves who did the housework. She told Themistocles the stories of gods and heroes and of the Battle of Troy. His father's occupation is not known, but all Athenians had some work in connection with the government of the city, work such as being responsible for a fleet, or being a juryman, directing a chorus, or building and sculpturing.

Themistocles had a spirit for doing things, certain kinds of things. He wasn't interested in being good-mannered or graceful, and he didn't learn to play the lyre. In Athens the mark of an uneducated man was "one who does not know how to play the lyre." But when Themistocles was called uneducated, he replied, "Although I don't play the lyre, yet I will bring greatness and glory to my city." When he had holidays from school, he did not spend them in play, but in inventing great orations about his city.

As he was growing up, he paid more and more attention to what was being discussed in the Agora and to the news that was passed from man to man about the whole Greek world, by now spread out in many colonies all around the Mediterranean Sea. He heard of the greatest city in Ionia, Miletus, and of a wise Greek named Thales who lived in Miletus.

Thales, who had learned from the Babylonians the science of the stars, had himself added new knowledge from his own studies of the laws of movement of the heavenly bodies. Out of this knowledge, he claimed that the moon sometimes comes between the sun and the earth and shadows the sun. He predicted an eclipse, when the day would be dark from this shadow. Some words of Thales which might have reached Themistocles' ears, and which he might have pondered, were, "God is the most ancient of all things, for He has no birth. The world is the most beautiful of all things, for it is the work of God. Time is the wisest of all things, for it finds out everything."

In 538 BC, perhaps a dozen years before Themistocles was born, the Persian King Cyrus had conquered Babylonia and allowed the captive Hebrews to return to their own land. Then he had led his armies westward to the Aegean Sea and took possession of all the lands along the eastern coast of that sea, including Miletus, one of many Greek cities in that part of the world. As part of the Persian Empire, the Greek colonies were ruled by Persian officials. Greeks had to serve in the Persian armies and supply the Persians with ships and sailors. Nevertheless, Cyrus was a good and fair conqueror.

In 529 BC, when Cyrus died, his son Darius became the new ruler of the Persian Empire. This was still a few years before Themistocles was born, but, by the time he was a grown man (499 BC), news reached Athens that the city of Miletus had revolted against Persian rule and wanted help from the Greek mainland. Sparta refused help, but Athens sent twenty ships loaded with warriors. When they reached Ionia, the Greeks marched northward to Sardis, a great Persian city in Lydia, and burned it to the ground. The enraged Darius swore to take vengeance on the Athenians and began by burning Miletus and destroying it entirely (494 BC). When this news reached Athens, everyone was stunned. A poet wrote a drama, "The Capture of Miletus," and when it was enacted, everyone wept.

Darius sent messengers to the mainland demanding gifts of earth and water as a sign that the Athenians would submit to him. Telling them to get the earth and water for themselves, Sparta and Athens threw the messengers into a pit and a well. Hearing of this, Darius ordered his armies into ships that crossed the Aegean to punish all who refused to submit by enslaving them and bringing them to Susa in Persia. All along their way, through the channel east of Attica, the Persians burned and destroyed all the cities that resisted them.

The Athenians gathered in the Agora and sent a runner to Sparta for help. He ran for two days and two nights without stopping. The Spartans promised help in five days, after they could make a sacrifice to Apollo at a full moon. Before the five days were up, the Persian fleet anchored in the bay at Marathon (490 BC), 26 miles north of Athens, and 26,000 Persian soldiers encamped on the plain which was surrounded by hills, with another 100,000 more Persians in boats as reserve troops.

Led by Miltiades, a general who had fought against the Persians in Ionia and who knew their ways, 9000 Athenian warriors, plus 1000 warriors from the nearby city of Plataea, marched to meet them and grouped their forces in the hills around the plain. Miltiades knew that the Persian line of attack was always strongest at the center, so he arranged his defense so that his line was strong at the wings and thinner at the center. When the Persians attacked at the center, the strong Athenian wings moved forward, closed in and surrounded the Persians. Only 192 Greeks were killed to 6400 Persians. The survivors fled to their ships and sailed away. Though his warriors were battle-weary, Miltiades led them straight back to Athens, for he guessed the Persians were heading there to take the undefended city. Sure enough, they arrived in time to face the Persian fleet once more.

Since the Athenians had sent to Sparta for help, now two thousand Spartan soldiers reached Athens. When the Persians saw the same Athenian army waiting to fight again, together with Spartan reinforcements, they finally sailed away for good.

The victory at Marathon came at a time when Themistocles was about 35 years old. He gloried in the great deeds of Miltiades, but he was certain this was not the end of war with Persia. He spoke up, persuading the Athenians that they must build more ships, improve the harbor at Athens and be ready for future trouble with the Persians. His voice began to be heard, and when it came, he would play a large part in meeting that trouble.

Darius, angered by the defeat at Marathon, called men from all over the Persian Empire to arms. Every day thereafter, and even after his death, Darius had a man who stood by the Persian throne and spoke the words, "Remember Marathon." For ten years troops gathered together and made preparations, but before the great expedition was ready, Darius died and his son Xerxes came to the throne. Xerxes went ahead with his father's plans to conquer Greece: "I will not cease until I have conquered Athens and burned it with fire."

This was a time when the whole Greek world was deciding what its future would be. Athens was ready, thanks to Themistocles, whose voice had been heard to build a better navy and a better harbor for Athens, and he was made admiral of the Athenian navy.

By 480 BC the Persians were ready to set out from Sardis. The plan was for the armies to march to the Hellespont (a large, strong river whose mouth was near ancient Troy) and cross it into Thrace (east of Greece), then move through Macedonia southward to Greece. The great multitude had to go by land, partly because the force was so large and partly because its soldiers were landsmen afraid of the sea and were unwilling to travel by ship. The Phoenicians, however, were seamen and their fleet was to join the army at the Hellespont and from there sail close to the shore to supply the army and to keep in touch with it as it marched on. There were perhaps 1200 ships in the fleet and 200,000 men in the army.

At the front of the march were the baggage bearers, men and horses. Then came the foot-soldiers in their ranks. Behind them a space was maintained to be followed by one thousand horsemen and one thousand spearmen, all of whom were Persian nobles. Ten sacred horses, wearing rich trappings, followed next. Then came the sacred chariot of the great Persian god. It was drawn by eight horses with the charioteer on foot, for no human was allowed to mount this chariot. Then came the Great King Xerxes, attended by spearmen from the best and most noble of all Persians. They were named the Immortals, of whom there were always 10,000 men, because if one died, he was replaced. They were the flower of the Persian army: 9000 carried spears ending in silver apples or pomegranates, 1000 held spears tipped with gold apples. Of all the nations who marched with Xerxes, the Persians wore the finest garments and much gold and bore as weapons: shields, daggers, bows and arrows. The ranks of Persians were followed by those from the reaches of the Persian Empire.

The Assyrians, wearing bronze helmets and linen breastplates, carried wooden clubs studded with iron. The Scythians, with pointed sheepskin caps, had battle-axes. The Caspians, dressed in skins, bore short swords. The Arabians in their loose robes carried long bows. The Ethiopians were dressed in leopard and lion skins, but in battle each man painted half of his body red and half white. On their heads they wore horses' scalps with ears and mane still attached, and they fought with a variety of weapons: long bows with sharp-pointed arrows, spears and clubs.

When the army met the Phoenician fleet at the Hellespont, Xerxes had a throne of white marble built for him. There he sat to direct the building of a bridge of boats across the strait, but before it could be crossed, a great storm arose and destroyed it. Xerxes, in fierce anger, ordered his soldiers to scourge the sea with 300 strokes of the lash, saying, "Thou bitter water, thy master lays on thee this penalty because thou didst wrong him, and Xerxes, the King, shall pass over thee whether thou be willing or no."

All the engineers who had built the bridge were beheaded, and a new bridge was built. At the rising of the sun, Xerxes prayed to the Sun as he poured an offering from a golden cup into the sea. He prayed that no accident would befall him before he had conquered all of the lands of the West. Then the army started to march over the bridge, and it took seven days and seven nights without pause.

The expedition then proceeded, and the fleet and the army met again at Therma, in sight of Mount Olympus and the mountains of Thessaly. All the towns through which the army passed were forced to provide food and drink for men and animals.

Meanwhile, the Greeks, led by Athens and Sparta, held a conference at Corinth. All the leading states except Argos and Thebes attended and agreed to serve under Sparta, to be united against the common foe.

In midsummer 480 BC, the Greeks marched to meet the Persians at Thermopylae, the narrow pass through the mountains between Thessaly and Greece. King Leonidas of Sparta, with only three hundred men, made ready to defend the pass. The rest of the Greek troops camped further south to defend the Isthmus of Corinth.

The Persian army camped before the pass. A Persian scout saw the Spartans practicing athletic exercises and combing their long hair, for "whenever they were about to put their lives in peril, they tended to the arrangement of their hair." The Persian fleet anchored at Artemisium. There were four times as many Persian ships as Greek. Xerxes planned to attack by land and sea at the same time; but a storm broke out at the moment of attack. It lasted three days and destroyed four hundred Persian ships. As the storm died down, the Greek ships commanded by Themistocles, attacked the Persians and defeated the Persian fleet.

Xerxes ordered his army to attack the pass. The Spartans held it for two days, and the Persians were driven back, many of them being killed. Xerxes watched the fighting from his marble throne. On the third day, a Greek traitor, a helot, bargained for gold with Xerxes and promised to lead the Persians along a mountain path so they could attack the Spartans from the rear. In the evening the Immortals set out with the traitor and followed him all night over the mountain and beyond the Spartan line. When scouts brought word to Leonidas that the Persians were in the rear, he knew then that the end had come. But he also knew that he commanded Spartan men and that while one remained alive, the pass would not be taken.

The Spartans were, however, attacked from the front, and they moved out into the open spaces so as to have more room to fight. They drove the Persians to the sea but were counter-attacked again and again. When Leonidas finally fell in battle, the Spartans fought for his body. Four times the Persians almost captured it, and four times the Spartans threw them back. Then word came that the Immortals were attacking from the rear. The remaining Spartans placed themselves around the body of Leonidas on a hill and defended themselves with daggers, for their spears were broken. Those who had no weapons left fought with their hands and teeth until all of them were cut down. Not a Spartan was left alive. They were buried where they fell. Only a few Spartan slaves lived to tell the story.

On a pillar, erected to their memory, were inscribed the words, "Stranger, bear word to the Spartans that we lie here obedient to their charge." Thus the Persians took the pass at Thermopylae, and the road to Athens lay clear before them.

The Athenian ships and good harbor could not protect Athens from the army of Xerxes, now advancing by land into Attica. The Athenians sent emissaries to Delphi to ask advice of the Oracle. The answer filled them with despair, for the Oracle told them that fire and the War-God were about to bring ruin upon them and that they must leave their homes and hide behind the walls of wood.

There was great discussion among the Greek generals as to the meaning of the Oracle. Some thought that a wooden fence should be built around the city, others that "walls of wood" could only mean the ships. Themistocles was of this opinion and he persuaded the people to forsake Athens and take refuge in the ships anchored near Salamis, an island off the coast of Athens. This they did, leaving a few men in the Acropolis to defend it.

The Persians soon entered Athens and attacked the Acropolis, so Athens and the Acropolis were both captured and burned to the ground. Themistocles had all the sick, the wounded, the women and children sent to Salamis. Near Salamis, the Athenian fleet had been joined by ships of the other Greek states, but at the news of the burning of Athens, all the other fleets decided to abandon the Athenians and sail for home. Themistocles tried to persuade them not to, but they only taunted him and said that the only reason he wanted to stay and fight at Salamis was because he now had no country. He replied that wherever there are Athenians and Athenian ships, there is Athens. Nevertheless the other Greek commanders were in favor of fleeing from the Persian ships.

It was then that Themistocles sent a message to Xerxes, pretending that he was now his ally. The message read that the Greeks were fighting among themselves and planning to sail away, and it advised Xerxes that if he would attack the Greeks before they escaped, he would win a great victory. Xerxes believed Themistocles, and at dawn the next day, he sent his great navy to attack the Greeks. Again the Great King Xerxes placed his throne where he could watch the maneuvering of the ships from the shore of Athens.

When faced with battle, the Greeks' fighting spirit rose and united them again. The Persians had the greater number of ships, but this did not help them; rather it was a hindrance, for the Greeks trapped the Persian fleet in the narrow strait between Athens and Salamis so that they could not turn around or help each other. In one day of fierce fighting the Greeks defeated the Persians. The sea became so full of wrecked ships and drowning men that "scarce any water could be seen."

It was now near the end of the summer, and Xerxes had news of a revolt back in Ionia. Following his defeat at Salamis, he sailed for Asia, leaving part of his army camped in Thessaly for the winter, so he would be ready to attack Greece again in the spring.

But when spring came and Xerxes tried to make a treaty with Athens, the Athenians refused. Knowing such a treaty would mean loss of freedom, the Spartans and Athenians went to fight the Persians at Plataea. The battle lasted all day. Mardonius, the Persian general, was killed. Without its leader, his army fled and were pursued by the Greeks who left few Persians alive.

When the victorious Greeks entered the Persian camp, they gazed in astonishment at the riches they found there. The tents were furnished with beds of gold and silver, with golden drinking cups and mixing bowls. One tenth of these riches were sent to Delphi and the rest divided among the Greek soldiers.

The Greeks found the tent of Xerxes, and King Pausanias of Sparta ordered Xerxes' cooks to prepare a meal such as they would for their master. Pausanias was dumbfounded to see the feast set down in the midst of gold and silver furnishings and richly colored curtains and covers. So, for fun, he ordered his own cooks to prepare a Spartan meal. He then called together all the Greek generals and pointed to the difference between the two meals, saying, "Hellenes, I have called you together to show you the senselessness of this leader of the Medes who, having such wealth as this, came to us who have such poor fare as this in order to take it away from us."

So Greece remained free, which proved that, in the cause of freedom, the weaker can stand against the stronger and prevail.

After the Persians were defeated, Themistocles became, for a time, the hero of all Greece. Wherever he went, people admired and applauded him by clapping their hands. So long as this went on, he felt that his great efforts for the Greeks were appreciated. He was happy and renewed in strength to make Athens strong again. Under his direction, men, women, and even children, worked willingly to rebuild Athens and erect a strong wall around the city. They also built a wall to protect the harbor, which was a few miles from the city, and to connect the harbor with the city by a Long Wall which formed a fortified road.

At length, Themistocles, fearing no new attack from the Persians, advised the Athenians that trade with the Persians would benefit and enrich Athens; but the Athenians could not accept his ideas now, and their feelings against him grew more and more bitter until at last they ostracized him (cast him out), and he had to leave his homeland, doomed to wander from place to place. Wherever he went, he was unwelcome. Athens had become a powerful state, and no other Greek city wanted to offend Athens by giving shelter to Themistocles. At last the only refuge he could find was with the new Persian ruler, Artaxerxes, in Susa.

Artaxerxes rejoiced when Themistocles begged his protection. The Greek hero now became his favorite, but the Persian King's courtiers called Themistocles "the Greek serpent," for they distrusted him.

Was Themistocles happy as the favorite companion of the Persian King, exiled from his beloved Athens? When Artaxerxes called upon Themistocles to help him in a new war against the Greeks, rather than do such a shameful deed, Themistocles drank poison and so put an end to his own life. He was loyal to his Greeks to the end.

Generations of Athenians looked back to all that Themistocles had done for Greece, recognized that he was a hero in the Persian Wars, and gratefully brought his body home to rest in a tomb beside that safe harbor which he had made for his city.

Pericles (499–429 BC)

After the Persian war, Greece was free again, but many Greek colonies in Asia were still under Persian rule. Many of the Greek leaders met on the small island of Delos, the birthplace of Apollo, and formed "The League of Delos," whose aim it was to free the Greeks in Asia and on the islands from Persia. Since the League needed money to build ships, each State that joined the League agreed to supply a certain sum of money each year. All these member states were at first free and equal. They took part in the work of the League and, one by one, the colonies were set free and joined the League. Athens was the leader, in charge of the money, although it was guarded in a treasury on Delos, and many of her laws were applied to the endeavors.

Over time, Athens acquired more and more power, and Athenians began to look on the other states as her subjects who must do whatever the Athenians wanted. Finally most of the states were almost ruled by Athens and became part of what some called the "Athenian Empire."

It was at this time that a great statesman was elected as *Strategus* (Planner) of Athens. His name was Pericles. Graceful and majestic in appearance, he was a noble whose concern was for the common people, for the poor as well as for the rich. He made it possible for every freeborn Athenian citizen to take an active part in the government, yet women and helots were not considered citizens. Every office was open to every citizen, and all officials were paid salaries by the state. Thus Athens became a limited democracy within herself, although she was tyrannical in relation to the states she controlled in the League of Delos.

Pericles was a great orator and was given the surname of "The Olympian." He was said to speak with thunder and lightning like Zeus. In one of his speeches, describing the Athenians, he said, "We are lovers of the beautiful, yet simple in our tastes, and we cultivate the mind without loss of manliness. We employ wealth when there is a real use for it, and we regard poverty as no disgrace. The disgrace is to do nothing to avoid it."

While Athens was being rebuilt after being burned by the Persians, Pericles inspired the Athenians to build some of the most beautiful temples and theaters in the world. On the Acropolis, a new Parthenon was designed by Ictinus and decorated with sculptures by Phidias, who also created the great 46-foot statue of Athena clad in gold that stood within the temple. The Athenians believed that Athena herself made her home in the Parthenon.

The theater of Dionysos was southeast of the Acropolis. Therein, plays were performed from sunrise to sunset at certain times of the year, and prizes were awarded to the best. Pericles made it possible for people who could not pay admission to enter the theater for free. Most of the plays were taken from legends of the gods and acted out by various individuals along with a chorus. The audience shouted applause to show approval, or groaned and hissed in disapproval of the plays or players. In a central space where the chorus stood was the altar to Dionysos, the god of wine and drama.

Many great men, whose names are still revered and whose works are still admired and performed in our time, lived during the Age of Pericles. Some of these men were the poets Aeschylus, Sophocles and Euripides. The great sculptors were Phidias and Polyclitus. There were also philosophers like Socrates and Anaxagoras. Each lived a life most true to his own nature, and all of them were encouraged by Pericles to do so.

It was Pericles' aim to make Athens the ruling city of the Greek world, but Sparta would have none of it. Sparta felt Athens had overstepped her authority and was threatening the Greek tradition of independent city-states. Two years before the death of Pericles, Sparta started a war against Athens which ended in the defeat of Athens.

At the end of the first year of the war, Pericles, in a funeral oration, made a comparison between the Spartans and the Athenians: "In respect to our training for war, we differ from our opponents, the Spartans, in several points. While the Spartans from earliest youth subject themselves to an irksome exercise for the attainment of courage, we with our easy habits of life are not less prepared than they to encounter all perils ... and we are gainers in the end by not vexing ourselves beforehand with sufferings to come, yet still appearing in the hour of trial not less daring than those who toil without ceasing." A year later Pericles died during an epidemic of a plague.

In the end, Athens was defeated by Sparta, and the Athenians were never able to regain the power they had enjoyed.

Education in Athens

All Athenian children began their education at home, where the girls remained until they married. The boys started school when they were seven years old, but they were not taken far away from home. They were placed under the charge of slaves, or pedagogs, who took them to school, carried their books, and helped them with lessons. The pedagogs were also expected to keep their pupils in good order, teach them good manners, answer all their many questions, and punish them when necessary. The schools opened at sunrise and closed before sunset, so that boys would not have to walk home through the dark and empty streets.

Having delivered his pupil to the school, the pedagog would wait all morning in the anteroom with all the other pedagogs. The school room was beyond. The boys sat on low benches with their writing tablets on their knees. The master sat on a higher chair in front of them. Musical instruments hung on the walls.

There were three main subjects in the school: letters, music and gymnastics, and arithmetic was taught as good training for the mind. With regard to learning numbers it was said, "Those who are born with a talent for arithmetic are quick at all learning, while even those who are slow at it have their general intelligence increased by studying it."

The pupils' first writing was done using styluses with sharp metal points on wood tablets that were covered with wax. When the students were able to write well enough, they were allowed to write on papyrus with reeds that were dipped in a sticky substance for ink. After learning, through writing, to understand what was written, the students were given the works of great poets to read as they sat on their benches in the school room. They had to learn many of these works by heart. Standing in front of their masters and repeating the lines after them, they hoped to become like the ancient heroes. Reciting poetry was not dull, for as they recited they acted it out.

After their lessons in letters and arithmetic, the school boys had their lessons in music; they learned to play the lyre and flute and to sing. The Athenians thought that music was a good medicine for all ills. One philosopher, when he was tired or annoyed, would play on his harp. "I am calming myself."

In the afternoon, the boys were taken by their pedagogs to the Palaestra, or wrestling school, for it was important to have a well-trained and graceful body. They spent the afternoons running, jumping, throwing the discus and javelin, and wrestling. Of course there were boys who preferred to play instead of work at their lessons. The usual punishment was a flogging given by the teacher with a strap to which was attached a cow's tail. This was called a "stinger." When flogged, the Athenian boys did not take it quietly but cried out loudly and begged for mercy.

The schooling lasted until a boy was eighteen, and throughout he gradually learned to feel enthusiasm for the greatness of his people and the freedom of their city and to grow in self-control, dignity and graceful action. At eighteen he left school and went into military training for a few years, after which he became a full citizen of Athens. Then he was given the shield and spear of a warrior, and, in the temple of Zeus before the highest magistrates, he took the oath of the *ephebi* (young men), which was: never to disgrace his holy arms, never to forsake his comrade in the ranks, to fight for the holy temples alone or with others, to leave the country not in a worse but in a better state than he found it, to obey the magistrates and the laws and defend them against attack and, finally, to hold in honor the religion of his country.

The education of Athenian girls was very different from the education of Spartan girls. While the Spartan girls were trained in wrestling, spear-throwing and other arts of war, the Athenian girls were in their homes learning the arts of creating a beautiful home and healthy family life. Among other things the girls learned to weave, embroider, and cook well, and to dance and make music. Some of the well-to-do families hired private tutors for their daughters, so those girls could learn to read and write. Basically women ran the home and were the social equals of their husbands at home. Outside the home, men and women operated in separate circles.

The result of the Athenian education produced many men of enormous creativity and capacity, from poets and great philosophers to playwrights and sculptors, from statesmen to scientists.

Priests of the Beautiful

We know the Athenians for their love of freedom. We also know them for their love of beauty. Because they reverenced the divinity dwelling in the human being, they also reverenced the beauty of the human body as an image of divinity. The gymnastics, the free-flowing clothing, the outdoor life all helped the Greeks to become the most beautiful race of men under the sun. Men were considered heroes because of their beauty, and after their death small shrines were raised in their memory, as if they were gods.

One time a slave was given the part of Dionysos in a play. He was so beautiful that, as he first appeared, the crowds applauded and his master immediately made him a free man. The Greek philosopher Isocrates said, "Virtue is honored only because it is moral beauty." And Plato said, "Beauty is the splendor of goodness."

Just as there were priests of Apollo and of Zeus, often chosen because of their beauty, so certain men appeared in Greece who, because they served beauty, might be called "priests of the beautiful." They were the poets and dramatists, the sculptors and architects, and the thinkers who were scientists and philosophers.

East and West

Like the golden tip of the pyramid of Khufu,
the Great King of the Persians shone for his people,
supported by them from below.
His word was the law and all beneath him
served him and upheld him.

The Greek temple is a picture of the Greek state,
with the columns standing side by side
to support the sloping roof,
just as the citizens stood side by side
to uphold the State that sheltered them.

Sophocles (c. 496–c. 406 BC)

When the Athenians held a great festival of thanksgiving after the victory at Salamis, there appeared a chorus of dancers who were young men of eighteen, *ephebi*. Among them was a young ephebus who was chosen for his great beauty to lead in the hymn of victory. His name was **SOPHOCLES**. All who looked upon him reverenced his fair beauty and felt as if they were beholding the image of a god.

Sophocles' father was a craftsman, the head of a great smithy where weapons of war were forged of iron. His home was among the olive groves in the valley of the River Cephisus, a part of the country where metals were abundant in the earth. As he grew up, Sophocles often stood on the crag of a steep mountain from which he had a view of the sea, the harbor at Piraeus, and Athens itself, with its white marble buildings gleaming in the sunshine.

Not much more is known about Sophocles until twelve years later, after the victory festival, when he again appeared before his fellow citizens, but this time not as an ephebus or as a soldier or because of his bodily beauty. This time he recited some verses of his own making at a festival for Dionysos. As the people gathered, they knew they were to hear a contest in poetry between this new young poet and one who was over sixty years old, one who had fought at

Marathon and Salamis and who had won a crown of laurel leaves many times in other contests. AESCHYLUS was his name. He had written a great poem about the war with the Persians and was already reverenced as the greatest poet in Athens. At this festival, then, Sophocles and Aeschylus competed by speaking each his own poem, and the people listened eagerly for the best. They gave the prize to Sophocles, who had composed a poem praising Attica as the home of a great people and as the center of a civilization which would spread to distant lands.

This was not the only time that Sophocles won first place in poetic competitions. EURIPIDES, a poet younger than Sophocles, was a third competitor. These three—Aeschylus, Sophocles and Euripides—are considered the greatest of the Greek playwrights, and their works were presented to the Greeks many years before the birth of Christ. Their plays have not been forgotten over the centuries since they lived. Their poetic dramas are about the tragedy of human imperfections, and they are still reverenced as among the greatest plays ever written and performed. Of the three poets, Sophocles was most beloved by the Athenians.

Phidias (c. 500–c. 432 BC)

The greatest sculptor of Greece was Phidias. When Athens was rebuilt after the Persians burned it down, Phidias chiseled the beautiful forms of gods to place in the temples he helped to build. He made two colossal statues, the one of Athena which was placed in her temple on the Acropolis, and one of Zeus for the temple at Olympia. According to the ancient writers, he had the greatest influence on the later sculptors. Polyclitus, one of his many pupils, formed figures of men in the most perfect attitudes and proportions. He made statues in bronze honoring athletes and heroes.

In their works of art, the Greeks were chiefly interested in portraying the human form. The classic Greek sculptures are more human than the older Egyptian statues which were often superhuman in size. The Egyptian sculptures of the head and form of a man seem to be seeing and listening to a world other than the human world. Most of them sit in meditation. In contrast, the statues of the classical Greek period are human in size, and their look is directed out into the world, although as yet their features are very beautiful but do not show human individuality. When looking at a Greek statue, one doesn't see any strong individual features shaping the face differently from other faces. One may speculate that in Greek statues one sees the ideal form of the human body and face, the pattern or model of all human form.

Phidias and his followers never used models for their sculptures. They knew from their own feelings how the limbs and head were formed. The artists had a strong sense for the shapes, movements, and relationships of the whole body. The sculptor was conscious of the form-giving forces of the gods, and this is what guided his chisel.

In the Greek statues one discovers something more than beauty of form and proportion, for they express a knowledge of the human being's inner powers—the powers of thinking, of feeling, and of will. In the Zeus statues, the quiet, erect head expresses wisdom. The Apollo statues portray a balance, a unity of limbs and body. There is no movement, no breath, but there is the smile in which we can see the shining of the heart. In one Amazon statue the element of breath is shown through the gesture of the arms, while the Hermes statues render expressions of the will in the movement of the graceful limbs.

Phidias was already an elderly man when he sculpted the *Parthenos*, as the statue of Athena in the Parthenon was called. This statue was 45 feet high, carved in ivory, and clothed in gold which was attached so that it could be removed and borrowed for the Athenian treasury in case of need. The goddess figure stood on a carved marble pedestal. The only light for the interior of the Parthenon came through a doorway to the east, and on Athena's feast day, the rising sun shone directly through the opening to illuminate her figure. Phidias, together with the architects Ictinus and Calicrates, worked on the building for nine years, from 447 to 438 BC.

The Birth of Philosophy

In the sixth century BC, in the city-state of Miletus, men began to ask questions that had never really been asked before. They asked what the basic stuff of life was. Where did people come from? How do we know what goodness is? They had many different answers which they discussed as they walked in the

Agora or marketplace. Some thought the basic stuff of life was water, some thought it was air or fire. Some thought we had once been fish who came out of the sea. No one really knew the answers, but they enjoyed arguing their points of view as a way to increase their understanding of human beings and life.

As time went on, this kind of questioning spread throughout the Greek world. One man, Pythagoras, thought numbers and form were the basis of life; others thought ideas were present even before numbers. These men became known as philosophers, which means "lovers of wisdom." Some of the greatest philosophers came from Athens: Socrates, Plato, and Aristotle.

SOCRATES (469–399 BC) was short, ugly and poor and cared not what people said about his habits or his looks. He spent his time in the Agora, and whenever he spoke, people stopped to listen. He went about barefoot and had only one cloak, so old that his friends made fun of it, but he was quite content, and said, "How many things there are which I do not want!"

His wife, Xanthippe, had a violent temper. Socrates commented, "One should live with a restless woman, just as horsemen have to manage violent-tempered horses, and once having mastered such a woman, then a man could easily manage others."

In the Agora, Socrates would talk to those who stopped to listen. He would ask questions mainly to demonstrate to people what real knowledge and thinking were. Often people will not admit that they don't know something, and when dealing with such people, Socrates would ask them so many questions that they would soon begin to contradict themselves and so end in a hopeless muddle. Some of them became angry. Others said, "Socrates makes me admit that my knowledge is worthless. I had best be silent, for I know nothing at all."

Socrates might ask, "Are you afraid of death?" The answer might be "Yes." Then he would ask, "Do you know what death is?" The answer, "No." Then he would add, "How can you be afraid of what you don't know?" He never really gave answers to his questions, and he never wrote down anything about his ideas.

Socrates believed that Truth was more important than any person, even than himself. Many men do not like to hear the truth when it is unpleasant; they would rather cover it up. Such men disliked Socrates. They said that his questioning was wicked and that he was an enemy of the State—and he was brought to trial as such. He made a great speech in defense of himself and affirmed that no fear of death could make him stop asking questions in his pursuit of truth.

Among the citizens who judged him at his trial, 281 voted that he should die as an enemy of the State. Only 220 voted that he was innocent. Eventually Socrates was given a cup that contained hemlock, a poisonous drink, and he took it quite cheerfully and calmly. Just before death, he spoke his last words to a friend who stood by him: "Crito, I owe a rooster to Aesculapius (the god of death). Do not forget to pay it."

The reason we know so much about Socrates is because of his student, PLATO (428/427– or 424/423–348/347 BC), one of the young men who followed Socrates and listened to him. Plato was a good note-taker. He wrote down everything that he could remember of the questions and conversations that Socrates had with those around him. These are recorded in his *Dialogues*.

Plato also started a famous school, the Academia, where young men could study philosophy. Plato was one of those who thought ideas came before anything else on earth was formed. He later wrote other works about politics, in which he described the kind of person who would make a good leader of people, a "philosopher king." Because he believed so strongly in what he called ideal forms, Plato lived deeply in his imagination and spent much of his time in contemplation. He also wrote a famous work called "The Cave," in which he suggests that there is an entire world of a spiritual nature that is infused with thoughts and light. He once said, "We can forgive a child who is afraid of the dark; the real tragedy is when men are afraid of the light."

One of Plato's students was a young man named ARISTOTLE (384–322 BC). As a teenager, he was sent to Athens to study at the Academia, and he stayed twenty years. Aristotle was interested in everything he could experience with his senses. He thought ideas came out of human experience: what people saw, heard and sensed in other ways. He thought that the more he could experience through his senses, the richer his knowledge and ideas would be, so he set off to do just that: to experience everything he could. He also liked to examine things closely, whether the thing was an animal or a play. He would sometimes make experiments to test his ideas about what he experienced. For this reason, he is often called the father of science. Aristotle was so gifted that Philip, the King of Macedonia, hired him to tutor his son in all that could be known in the world. This young man grew up to become Alexander the Great.

Aristotle also wrote about how to become a good person by doing our best in every way. He said, "We are what we repeatedly do. Excellence, then, is not an act, but a habit."

Although he disagreed with much of what Plato thought, he loved his teacher deeply, and he did not start a school of his own until after Plato died. Then Aristotle started a new school in Athens, the Lyceum. Here he and his pupils researched the known world in as much detail as they could. Aristotle gave us an amazing wealth of information about the world and the times in which he lived. Among the things he wrote about were plants, animals, geography, politics, weather, literature, medicine, and history.

Socrates, Plato, and Aristotle gave the world great gifts. Their work is still studied in universities today because it is so stimulating. All three of these men inspire us to be thoughtful and thorough, and to bring our best to everything we do, so that we can be full human beings.

After Pericles

"Anyone coming from abroad and seeing Greece today would regard us as great fools, struggling among ourselves about trifles and destroying our own land when we might, without danger, conquer all of Asia." These were the words of Isocrates, the Greek orator. Isocrates was nine years old when Pericles died. When he was old, he was one of several elders who, about seventy years after Pericles' death, still remembered seeing Pericles when they were little boys.

Athens had changed. Her citizens were now more interested in their private affairs than in public affairs. They engaged in much trade with the East in order to make money. There was no longer a citizen army but a paid army or militia. The spirit of Athens was weak because of defeat in wars with other Greek states, among them Thebes, Corinth and Sparta. Pericles had tried to join them together with Athens in a federation of states, and Sparta did just that, forming the Peloponnesian League. These other states became jealous of

Athens and, led by Sparta, made war on her. Pericles died in a great plague soon after the war started, and Athens had no great leader to replace him.

Sparta became, for the next thirty years, the leader of Greece and allied itself with Persia. At length a great general, Epaminondas of Thebes, led a revolt against Sparta and defeated the Spartans, but he was killed. Without him the Thebans could not hold Greece together, and she became a country divided into many camps, each one ready to fight the other and helpless against any greater power. Yet the Greeks and their culture had spread all over the Mediterranean world. The Greek language, the Greek gods and their temples, Greek books, pottery, art and furniture had spread throughout their world.

When a greater leader did come, this time it was not from the East but from the north.

Philip of Macedon (359–336 bc)

Macedon, the mountain country to the north of Greece, was ruled by King Philip, who received a Greek education and studied the arts of war with Greek teachers. Philip looked toward Greece with the one great aim of uniting it, for he had deep respect for the Greek spirit and culture, especially the Athenians. He even married a Greek priestess. Philip raised a strong army of peasant soldiers and marched into Greece.

In Athens, two parties arose: one for Philip led by Isocrates and one led by Demosthenes (c. 384–322 bc), who tried to persuade people to resist the Macedonian. His speeches against Philip are knows as the "Philippics."

As a child, Demosthenes stammered. Yet he grew up with a passion for oratory, or public speaking. As a boy, he would go to listen to all the most noted orators; then he would go home afterwards to practice the art of oration by himself. The first time he spoke in public, everyone laughed at his stammering and his weak voice. He determined to overcome his difficulties and built himself a place underground to work. Here he would force himself to stay for two or three months at a time by shaving one-half of his head so that shame would keep him in.

He disciplined his voice and overcame his stammer by speaking with pebbles in his mouth and by reciting verses while he was out of breath from running or by climbing while he spoke. He would stand in front of a looking glass to watch his own gestures. To cure himself of the habit of raising his left shoulder while speaking, he stood under a hanging sword-point. During storms he went down by the sea and tried to make his voice heard above the storm so as to get used to the noise of the public assembly. Through his self-training and discipline, he became one of the greatest of Greek orators.

Demosthenes was for a free city-state while Philip represented monarchy, rule by a king. Demosthenes compared Philip to a wolf and a bloodsucker, and he called for a citizen army to rise up and fight. He led this army against the Macedonians, but Philip tricked Demosthenes' army, and got behind it, defeated it, and marched into Thebes. After this defeat, the Athenians turned against Demosthenes, hissed at him in the streets, and called him "the Snake."

As conqueror, Philip did not act as the Spartans had. He called a council of all Greek cities at Corinth and formed the Hellenic League. Each city could have its own council, its own government, which he would not interfere with except in time of war. He did not ask to be called King of Greece but only "Captain-General." The only Greek city which did not join this league was Sparta, which refused, saying, "We are accustomed to lead, not to be led." Then Philip stated his real aim: to lead the Greeks and his own Macedonians against Persia and "free the seas, liberate the Greek cities in Asia, and restore Hellas [Greece] to its true grandeur." Now all welcomed him as a great leader—except Demosthenes, who decided to leave Greece forever rather than endure the end of democracy in the land he loved.

Having accomplished the union of Greece as one league under his leadership, Philip went back to Macedon to celebrate and give his troops some rest before setting forth on his planned expedition against Persia. Then, just as he was most triumphant, in the midst of his celebrations, just as he stepped out of his great hall to the sound of trumpets, a bareheaded man ran up behind him, screaming with hate, and stabbed him in the back with a knife so that he fell dead.

The next day, people (merchants, agents, couriers, spies) slipped southward along the mountain roads carrying the news of Philip's death into Greece. Now it was not as if a ship had lost its captain but rather as if a ship, half built on the shore, had lost its builder. What was to happen next?

In his speeches against Philip, Demosthenes had often quoted a verse which the Oracle at Delphi had given him:

> *The eagles shall see, watching from the skies,*
> *The conquered weep, while a conqueror dies.*

Alexander the Great (356–323 BC)

King Philip's son, Alexander, was twenty years old when his father died. He had the beauty of a young Greek god, a brilliant mind and great personal charm. Aristotle himself had been one of his teachers. He now succeeded Philip on the throne.

The Macedonians were horse breeders. When Alexander was a boy, some horse traders from Greece were showing Philip a string of colts and putting them through their paces. The King was selecting the best of the animals for his cavalry.

Alexander was watching and noticed that one horse gave constant trouble. It was black except for a white, starry mark on its forehead. It tossed and pulled at its halter and backed away from the men who tried to examine it. It swirled and circled, bit and kicked; it wouldn't let anyone mount it, rearing and throwing off all who tried. Shouting, men crowded around it. Alexander noticed the horse's distress and over-excitement. Philip's horse inspectors said it was too savage to train, but Alexander felt a longing for it. The inspectors rejected it, but Alexander ran over to them, shouting, "You mustn't lose that horse." No one paid much attention to the boy. Again he cried, "It's the finest horse, and you just don't know how to manage him."

"Are you telling me the inspectors can't manage that colt?" asked Philip.

Alexander was desperate and said, "I can manage this horse. I can bring him under my hand." And so he did! To the amazement of the King and his men, Alexander walked quietly to the horse. Talking gently, he turned the horse toward the sun, so it wouldn't be frightened by shadows. Alexander waited till the horse began to graze, then jumped on its back, and let it run without drawing it in, until the horse was so tired out it was no longer wild. The onlookers were impressed that Alexander could stay on the beast as it galloped and tried to buck the boy off. So Philip gave the horse to Alexander. Alexander named him Bucephalus (Ox-Head) because of its great head and stubbornness.

Bucephalus was one of three loves in Alexander's life. The other two were a copy of *The Iliad* and his teacher, Aristotle, who gave him the copy of *The Iliad*. Alexander would read *The Iliad* at night, although he knew most of it by heart, and then place the book in a golden box, also from Aristotle, under his wooden headrest when he slept. He thought a lot about Achilles and actually later took the nickname Achilles.

Aristotle had come from Athens to tutor Alexander and other friends close to him. He taught the boys in a deserted temple. In the temple, instead of figures of the gods, were all kinds of things: piles of various kinds of rocks, boxes of shellfish, stuffed birds, insects, a basin of living fish, books of butterflies, pressed leaves, and collections of many other living and growing things. These they studied. Every morning at daylight, before going to Aristotle's Academy, Alexander made a sacrifice to Zeus.

From the study of things near at hand, the new approach to study that Aristotle had brought into the world, the students progressed to a study of far-off places. Alexander discovered that beyond the known East were other unknown lands, where the great rivers had their origins in high mountains.

Aristotle did not mention the gods nor did he deny them. Alexander believed that the true gods might be found beyond Babylon (which means "the Gate of God"), since travelers had by now climbed Mount Olympus and found nothing but bare rock at its summit. Somehow he imagined a wall of mountains, higher than any others and toward the east, beyond which lived the gods, the creators of the wonders of life. Alexander revered Aristotle and would say, "From my father I received life; from Aristotle I learned to lead a good life."

As King of Macedon, Alexander wanted to carry out his father's plans to not only unite Greece but also the whole known world, and to try to find the home of the gods on earth.

When Thebes revolted against Alexander's rule over Greece, he put down the revolt by burning and destroying the whole city except for the house of Pindar, a poet.

Then he gathered together a mighty army of Macedonians and Greeks. This army was never to know defeat for, like his father, Alexander was a great military genius. With his army recruited, he sent a message to the Persian king: "I, Alexander, consider the whole of thy treasure, the whole of thy land, to be mine."

The army numbered 25,000 men, one-half of all the men in Macedon plus a paid division of Athenian foot-soldiers. The cavalry from Thessaly brought the size of the army to 30,000. In addition to the fighting men, there were two surveyors to map the journeys, a mineralogist to collect specimens of rocks, a weather expert, and other scientists who were to keep a record of all animal and plant life. There were Greek political leaders and even a collection of exotic animals. Alexander also carried a notebook in which to keep a journal. His friends asked, "Are you taking an army along or an academy? Is this an exploring expedition or an invasion?" It was both.

Finally all was ready, and the long columns of soldiers and horsemen set out, with Alexander walking in the dust along with the foot-soldiers, and with the black horse, Bucephalus, led behind him. As they marched, Alexander's mind dwelt on the old story of Agamemnon and the Greek heroes who, so long ago, had marched against Troy. He, too, was at last on his way to Troy.

Once there, he camped below the ruined towers of Troy, on the plain where the Greeks and Trojans had fought their mighty battles. There he erected altars to Zeus and worshiped at the temple of Athena, and sacrificed and prayed for the success of his cause. Over the years, from among the ruins, people had gathered broken bits of spears and armor. The attendants in Athena's temple showed him a shield which they said had been Achilles'. Alexander took this with him, leaving his own in its place. He paid a visit to the tomb of Achilles and placed a wreath on it.

As Alexander's army advanced to the east of Troy, toward the Granicus River, it came upon an army of the Great Persian King: thousands of heavily armed Greek foot-soldiers hired from among the Asiatic Greeks by the Persian

King, and troops of Persian horsemen wearing loose trousers and colored capes and carrying small shields and sheaves of javelins slung at their hips.

The Macedonians attacked. Alexander, at the head of his army, was the first to plunge into the river and into the thick of battle. The Asiatics scattered, but in the battle Alexander was struck on his helmet by a sword, and he lost his vision for a moment from the shock. A Persian chief in golden armor struck at him again and would have killed him but for Clitus, his bodyguard, who saved Alexander's life by cutting off the chief's arm. The Persians were routed and disappeared as quickly as they had appeared.

This was Alexander's first victory, to be followed by many more. Fearlessly leading his troops, in every battle he was at the front, in the most dangerous spots. Marching south, he freed the Greek cities one by one. He moved along the coast, then looped north again, and east; then he went south to the Gulf of Issus and freed all western Asia from the Persian yoke. The people hailed him as a god. But the main Persian army had not as yet appeared.

Then, at Issus, it did appear, led by the Great King, Darius III himself. Alexander, on Bucephalus, led his cavalry in an attack on one end of the Persian line to get behind it and drive it toward his own infantry. The Persians fled in disorder across the Euphrates River, and Darius sought an agreement to make the Euphrates the boundary of his Empire. Alexander's advisors suggested to him that Philip's aims had been accomplished, that enough of a conquest had been made. But Alexander had other ideas and pushed on south along the eastern Mediterranean, thus to deprive the Persian fleet of all its harbors.

He made his way to the Nile River and Egypt, which he had no trouble taking from the Persians who were its rulers at that time. There he stayed to plan and start a city at the most western part of the mouth of the Nile. He called it Alexandria! From this city he would be in a position to control the ships that sailed the Mediterranean Sea.

In Egypt, Alexander visited the great temples that had been built thousands of years before his time. He visited the pyramids and the other Egyptian tombs and saw the picture writing on the walls of their chambers. He learned about Ammon-Re, the Sun-God, and about Osiris. In his mind Ammon-Re and Zeus were the same, as were Apollo and Osiris.

Alexander went out into the western desert to an oasis to visit the Temple of Ammon-Re. The priests welcomed him and let him enter. He was in the dark shrine alone, and when he emerged, the priests pronounced him "the son of Zeus-Ammon," and thus in part a god. After that he was considered a Pharaoh of Egypt. Wherever he went, the Egyptians knelt to him, for to them the Pharaoh was a god.

Meanwhile, the plans for Alexandria were developed further to include not only a harbor and lighthouse, but an academy, a temple, a gymnasium, a sports arena, and a library.

Leaving a political governor as his representative in Egypt, Alexander moved northward again in pursuit of the Persian King. He crossed the Tigris River, and on a plain below the mounds which covered the ruins of Nineveh, the Persian Emperor would make his last stand against Alexander. Darius had rigged his war chariots with scythes, and his soldiers outnumbered the Macedonians. But they could not defend themselves against Alexander's tactics in battle and were easily defeated. Alexander pursued Darius as he fled, but only caught up with him much later after he had been assassinated by some of his own men for being a coward.

Thus ended the Persian Empire, which now became the Empire of Alexander the Great, Captain-General of Hellas, Pharaoh of Egypt—and now the Great King of Persia.

As the new Great King, he marched into Babylon through wide, fertile gardens irrigated with water pumped up from the Euphrates. He was met by a procession of priests bearing rich gifts. They escorted him through the streets and past the great temple towers erected in olden times of sun-baked brick, towers that approached the Babylonian gods and the stars of heaven—such as the Tower of Bab-El, "the Gate of the Lord." Here in Babylon, Alexander found a library filled with books made of clay and covered with wedge-shaped writing. He made Babylon his capital city and, leaving a governor in charge as he had done elsewhere, he continued eastward to Persepolis, the capital of the ancient Persian kingdom on the Persian plateau.

Here, Alexander took up his abode in the rich palace of the Persian kings. This was the palace from which Xerxes, himself, had set forth to conquer Greece.

As a symbol of his victory, Alexander set fire to the palace, as revenge for the burning of Miletus and Athens, but did not destroy it.

Then, as he explored parts of Persia, Alexander found stores of treasure including Athenian sculptures, all of which he claimed and sent back to Greece. He discovered that the temples of Persia were stone altars on high places where fire burned day and night. When he questioned the priests who attended these altar-fires, they told him they were worshipers of Ahura Mazda, who shared in the power of the Sun and who was to be found in light and on the high places. The priests described the human being as struggling through all eternity to raise himself out of the darkness to the light and to free himself from evil and lift himself to the good.

Then the priests told Alexander the legend of Mithra, the son of Ahura Mazda, born in the night of the Winter Solstice in a cavern or grotto that was situated on earth between the two constellations of stars in the heavens known as the Ox and the Ass. This birth had come to pass at the time when the constellation known as the Virgin was highest in the sky.

Alexander could see that Ahura Mazda was like the Greek Zeus, the Father-God, and that Mithra was like Dionysos. It seemed to Alexander that the Persian Magi, or wisemen, had drawn their wisdom from the same knowledge as the ancient Greeks. He noticed that Zend, the language of the Holy Avesta, the Persian sacred hymns, was similar to the Greek language, and so he was convinced that sometime in the past the Greeks and the Persians must have been related.

Alexander then visited the solitary tombs of the Persian Kings: of Cyrus who had conquered Croesus, of Darius who had burned Miletus, and of Xerxes who had burned Athens. These tombs were out among the pastures where herds of sheep were grazing. No people lived near. The tombs were white, decorated only with a sun disk between eagle wings. There was a single altar fire attended by the priests. They told Alexander that here, in this peaceful region, there had been no war for two hundred years. He told them to remain in attendance and promised not to let them be attacked or harmed.

Now Alexander's mind concerned itself with what lay yet further beyond the rising sun. In Persia he had seen, amid the treasure, bags of gold dust marked "From the lands of the Indus." Those lands, he learned, lay to the east where rose a ridge of mountains called the Great Wall, and from whose snows flowed the Indus River. The Persian Magi had told him that along this river, other descendants of Persia called Aryans dwelt. They said that if he kept on to the east, he would find himself on the track of an ancient Aryan migration that passed to this unknown east centuries ago.

The story of how Alexander led his men over the earth's top (in what is Afghanistan today) is the story of his greatest adventure. He not only had to fight fierce mountaineers, who had never been conquered before, but he had to fight against cold, starvation, thirst, and later the desert. The Macedonians climbed higher each day and won their way against all resistance over a period of two and a half years. So Alexander passed, after marching 3900 miles since his first sight of the mountains, through the Khyber Pass and into the valley of the Indus River. He did not find the home of the gods on earth, as he had hoped, but instead an immense land of great beauty which was swarming with human beings.

He found people who spoke Greek and who said they were descendants of those who had followed Dionysos in his wanderings over the earth. He found ivy and laurel groves which he hadn't seen since leaving home. He saw ever higher mountain ranges, called the Himalayas today, which, guides said, were the greatest of heights and were guarded by the god Indra, who dwelt in the upper air amid the storms. So high were these mountains that Alexander knew no army could ever get over them, so he turned south to follow the Indus River toward the sea.

Many men had followed Alexander through these hardships without complaint. They were very faithful to him, although many had long since wanted to turn back. Now, even the faithful wanted to go back to the West. It had been ten years since his Macedonians had seen their wives and children.

Just at this time, a book was brought to Alexander from Greece. It was one that Aristotle had written since Alexander had left Macedon. Alexander read it eagerly. Aristotle said, "Not on this earth but only in the realm of the outermost stars does the Creator exist. The Power that revolves the stars around the earth moves all things else." And now, Alexander admitted to himself that he could see the gods and could meet with nothing but natural things in his journey. Thus were his followers finally able to convince him to turn back.

He and his men sailed down the Indus River to the Indian Ocean. In the process he conquered many people and at one point was struck by an arrow in the chest. Yet he continued to march along the coasts to make his way back to Babylon. In spite of this, something of the East had taken hold of him, just as he had brought Greek people and things to the East.

He was considered divine by the Egyptians and the Persians, but among the Indians, was one old man who scorned him. This old man joined Alexander's company with no possessions other than a mat to sit on and a begging bowl. He said, "You have taken much and destroyed much. Look at what you wear on your back and be fearful for yourself. It is not by what you wear or own that you will live henceforth. You have troubled much of the earth, but you own no more of it than that which will cover your body when you die."

It had taken Alexander twelve years to accomplish his goals. Now, as Great King, he had almost become a Persian. He had a Persian wife, and he placed Persians on equal terms with Macedonians. People bowed and prostrated themselves before him and kissed his feet. No longer was he the friend and leader of his own men. They too had to kiss his feet. This was not the Greek way, and they did not like him as Great King. They could not criticize him as in the old days.

One by one, his old friends plotted against him, and Alexander had them tried and executed. Clitus, who had once saved his life, criticized him for these executions, and Alexander, in a drunken rage, killed Clitus. Following this Alexander was speechless with grief; he refused to eat, and his officers had to prevent him from taking his own life. Callisthenes, the nephew of Aristotle, was among those executed, and thus Alexander became estranged from his beloved teacher as well.

In the midst of this strange change of character, while he was planning to add Arabia and lands west of Greece to his Empire, Alexander became ill with a fever which became steadily worse, and finally he died. He was only 33 years old. As he lay dying, his men filed past him in grief. When he was asked who should succeed him as ruler, he answered, "The strongest."

In less than twelve years, as explorer-conqueror, Alexander had carried Greek civilization to the very heart of Asia. The age which followed his death became known as the Hellenistic Age, and Alexandria, in Egypt, became its leading city. The Greek language was now spoken in Egypt and Asia. Greece, herself had weakened within and never again rose to be a great state, but the Greek "spirit" prevailed and pervaded the history of Western civilization.

This spirit included: Love of Truth, Love of Freedom and Love of Beauty. The greatness of the Greeks lay not only in what they did or did not do, but also in their spirit which searched for freedom, truth and beauty. They fought for their freedom against Persia, yet so loved the freedom of the individual city-states that they could not unite even among themselves. Their love of truth was expressed by people like Socrates, Plato, and Aristotle, who were among the greatest Greek searchers after truth. Their love of beauty can still be seen in the works of Greek pottery and art, the statues and temples, the dramas and songs which continue to inspire us to this day.

The Greeks gave us the Olympic Games, the basis of our alphabet, the first explorations into democracy, a new kind of thinking in philosophy, the birth of science and history, and the spirit of moral inquiry. All this continues to live on in the Western world today.

⌒

People today can be very grateful for the gifts that have some down to us from ancient history. Much of who we are today rests in the accomplishments and ideas of the people of the ancient world. By studying ancient history, we can broaden who we are and be inspired to live up to the examples of the great individuals who lived so long ago.

Bibliography

Ancient India

Arnold, Edwin. *The Light of Asia, Light of the World.* E-Art New Books: e-artnow.org, 2015.

Coomaraswamy, Ananda Kentish and Sister Nivedita. *Myths of the Hindus and Buddhists.* New York: Dover Publications, 1967.

Dutt, Romesh C., trans. *The Mahabharata and Ramayana: The Epic of Ancient India Condensed into English Verse.* New York: Everyman's Library, E.P. Dutton, 1944; Lulu Press, 2013.

Mackenzie, Donald A. *Indian Myth and Legend.* London: New Age Books, 2000.

Macnicol, Nicol, ed. *Hindu Scriptures.* New York: Everyman's Library, E.P. Dutton, 1943.

Menen, Aubrey. *The Ramayana.* New York: Charles Scribner's Sons, 1954.

Müller, F. Max, ed., "Laws of Manu" from *The Sacred Books of the East*, Vol. XXV. Oxford University Press: www.holybooks.com/the-sacred-books-of-the-east-all 50 volumes.

Potter, Charles Francis. *The Great Religious Leaders.* New York: Simon and Schuster, Tobermony Books, 1958.

Sayings of Buddha. New York: Peter Pauper Press, 1957.

Thomas, Henry and Dana L. *Living Biographies of Religious Leaders.* Garden City, NY: Garden City Publishing Co., 1942; Blackstone Audio, Inc., 2006.

Ancient Persia

Müller, F. Max, ed. "The Zend-Avesta" from *The Sacred Books of the East*, Vol. IV, trans. James Darmesteter. Oxford: Clarendon Press, 1895; www.holybooks.com/the-sacred-books-of-the-east-all 50 volumes.

Potter, Charles Francis. *The Great Religious Leaders*. New York: Simon and Schuster, 1958.

Thomas, Henry and Dana L. *Living Biographies of Religious Leaders*. Garden City, NY: Garden City Publishing Co., 1942; Blackstone Audio, Inc., 2006.

Mesopotamia

Breasted, James Henry. *Ancient Times: A History of the Early World*. Boston: Ginn and Company, 1916.

Bryson, Bernarda. *Gilgamesh*. New York: Henry Holt Co., 1967; revised edition illustrated by Reg Down, Createspace Independent Publishing, 2012.

Cornfeld, Gaalyahn, ed. *Adam to Daniel: Illustrated Guide to the Old Testament*. New York: MacMillan Co., 1961.

Creighton, David. *Deeds of Gods and Heroes*. London: St. Martin's Press, MacMillan Publishers, 1967.

Goodrich, Norma Lorre. *The Ancient Myths*, a Mentor Book. New York: The New American Library, 1960.

Herget, H.M. *Everyday Life in Ancient Times: Highlights of the Beginnings of Western Civilization in Mesopotamia, Egypt, Greece and Rome*. Washington, DC: National Geographic Society, 1953.

Meador, Betty De Shong. *Inanna: Lady of Largest Heart:Poems of the Sumerian High Priestess Enheduanna*.Austin: University of Texas Press, 2000.

Mills, Dorothy. *Book of the Ancient World.* Kettering, OH: Angelico Press, 2007.

Ragozin, Zenaide A. *Assyria,* The Story of the Nations series. New York: G.P. Putnam's Sons, 1887–1888.

————. *Chaldea: From the Earliest Times to the Rise of Assyria,* The Story of the Nations series. New York: G.P. Putnam's Sons, 1887–1888.

————. *Media, Babylon and Persia,* The Story of the Nations series. New York: G.P. Putnam's Sons, 1887–1888.

Steiner, Rudolf. *Occult History: Historical Personalities and Events in the Light of Spiritual Science.* London: Anthroposophical Publishing Co., 1957; Forest Row, UK: Rudolf Steiner Press, 1982.

Tolstoy, Leo. *Fables and Fairy Tales.* trans. by Ann Dunnigan, New York: The New American Library, 1962; Penguin Group, 1972.

Ancient Egypt

Baumann, Hans. *The World of the Pharaohs of Egypt.* New York: Pantheon Books, 1960.

Breasted, James Henry. *Ancient Times: A History of the Early World.* Boston: Ginn and Company, 1916.

Creighton, David. *Deeds of Gods and Heroes.* London: St. Martin's Press, MacMillan Publishers, 1967.

Herget, H.M. *Everyday Life in Ancient Times: Highlights of the Beginnings of Western Civilization in Mesopotamia, Egypt, Greece and Rome.* Washington, DC: National Geographic Society, 1953.

Ludwig, Emil. *The Nile: The Life Story of a River.* Whitefish, MT: Literary Licensing, 2013.

Merry, Eleanor C. *The Ascent of Man,* Classics of Anthroposophy series. Edinburgh, UK: Floris Books, 2008.

Prideaux, Tom and Josephine Mayer. *Never to Die: The Egyptians in Their Own Words,* a poetry anthology. New York: Viking, 1938; Whitefish, MT: Kessinger Publishing, 2003.

Steiner, Rudolf. *Egyptian Myths and Mysteries: 12 Lectures.* trans. Norman Macbeth, Great Barrington, MA: SteinerBooks, 1990.

Ancient and Early Greece

Aldington, Richard, trans. *The Larousse Encyclopedia of Mythology.* Introduction by Robert Graves. Amherst, NY: Prometheus Books, 1971; also New York: Barnes & Noble, 1994.

Breasted, James Henry. *Ancient Times: A History of the Early World.* Boston: Ginn and Company, 1916.

Bury, John Bagnell. *History of Greece to the Death of Alexander the Great*, volume 1. London: MacMillan, 1900.

Colum, Padraic. *Children's Homer: The Adventures of Odysseus and a Tale of Troy.* New York: Simon and Schuster, 2004.

Creighton, David. *Deeds of Gods and Heroes.* London: St. Martin's Press, MacMillan Publishers, 1967.

Eliot, Alexander. *A Concise History of Greece.* New York: Time, Inc., Life World Library, 1965; London: Cassell, 1972.

Guerber, H.A. *Myths of Greece and Rome.* North Chelmsford, MA: Courier Corporation, 1907; also Redditch, UK: Read Books, 2013.

Herget, H.M. *Everyday Life in Ancient Times: Highlights of the Beginnings of Western Civilization in Mesopotamia, Egypt, Greece and Rome.* Washington, DC: National Geographic Society, 1953.

Lamb, Harold. *Alexander of Macedon: The Journey to World's End.* New York: Doubleday, 1957.

Mills, Dorothy. *The Book of the Ancient Greeks.* Kettering, OH: Angelico Press, 2007.

Schuré, Édouard. *The Great Initiates: A Study of the Secret History of Religions.* Great Barrington, MA: SteinerBooks, 1992.

Steiner, Rudolf. *Education as an Art.* Great Barrington, MA: SteinerBooks, 1988.

————. *Wonders of the World: Trials of the Soul and Revelations of the Spirit*, 10 lectures (Munich 1911), Forest Row, UK: Rudolf Steiner Press, 1983.

Elizabeth Gardner Lombardi's Recollections of Dorothy Harrer:

I was privileged to have Dorothy Harrer as a teacher for three years at the Rudolf Steiner School in New York City from fourth grade through sixth grade during the 1940s. Mrs. Harrer took many classes through eight years as a class teacher, but this was her first class, and I was very aware or her working hard to prepare lessons. She had taught previously in a poor section of Appalachia where one of her students confided in her about experiences with elementals. She herself had a genuine relationship with the spirit.

Brought up in India as a child, she made the myths and history of that country very alive for our class. This was also true of her sharing tales from ancient Egypt and Greece. She had both a talent for the English language and a gift for drawing. She also had a talent for appreciating the gifts of each child, not only encouraging us, but also challenging us to expand our expectations.

Dorothy and her husband William founded Camp Glen Brook, 250 acres of farmland and forests in the New Hampshire mountains where students from the City could experience the calming influence of nature without media. Camp included crafts, music, drama, sports and hiking. Dorothy's special domain was the care of the animals. Sunday mornings the entire camp would convene for singing and an inspiring story.

The Harrers bequeathed this property to the Garden City Waldorf School, NY, whose students and adults visit often, working side by side to tend the farm animals, maintain buildings and grounds and complete whatever chores this rural setting requires, where children come to appreciate their own imaginations, the company of others, and the wonders of the natural world.

In the years I knew the Harrers, there were no teacher training centers in the US, and teachers helped each other and studied what had been written for the first Waldorf School teachers in Stuttgart, Germany. One could say that Dorothy Harrer was one of the pioneer class teachers. She was responsible for much of the early literature published in English about the Waldorf curriculum. Her books are still widely used in Waldorf schools in English-speaking countries.

Mrs. Lombardi herself had no formal training when she became a Waldorf teacher a year after graduating from Oberlin College, OH, though by that time there were three schools in the US following Steiner's pedagogical indications.

47855022R00086

Made in the USA
Middletown, DE
03 September 2017